# THE
# SPIRITUALITY
# OF
# GENTLENESS

*Growing
Toward Christian
Wholeness*

JUDITH C. LECHMAN

*A Ruth Graham Dienert Book*

1817

**Harper & Row, Publishers, San Francisco**

New York, Cambridge, Philadelphia, St. Louis
London, Singapore, Sydney, Tokyo

THE SPIRITUALITY OF GENTLENESS. Copyright © 1987 by Judith C. Lechman. All rights reserved. Printed in the United States of America. No part of this book may be used or reproduced in any manner whatsoever without written permission except in the case of brief quotations embodied in critical articles and reviews. For information address Harper & Row, Publishers, Inc., 10 East 53rd Street, New York, N.Y. 10022. Published simultaneously in Canada by Fitzhenry & Whiteside Limited, Toronto.
FIRST HARPER & ROW PAPERBACK EDITION PUBLISHED IN 1989.

Library of Congress Cataloging-in-Publication Data

Lechman, Judith C.
    The spirituality of gentleness.

    Includes index.
    1. Spiritual life.    I. Title.
BV4501.2.L42   1987        241'.4        86-45816
ISBN  0-06-065221-7
ISBN  0-06-065234-9 (pbk.)

88  89  90  91  92  93  BANTA  10  9  8  7  6  5  4  3  2  1

*To Bern,*
*the gentlest of companions along the Way*

# Contents

I would like to express my gratitude
and deepest appreciation for the encouragement
and support of Charlotta Stewart, Jim Lenhart,
Roy M. Carlisle, Ruth Graham Dienert, and Betti Colucci
in the writing of this book.

# INTRODUCTION:
# To Grow in Gentleness

I am the true vine, and my Father is the vinedresser. Every branch of mine that bears no fruit, he takes away, and every branch that does bear fruit, he prunes, that it may bear more fruit.

—JOHN 15:1–2

Gentleness isn't attractive to us. We equate it with weakness and lack of courage. Ponder gentleness and the mind's eye conjures up disdainful pictures of surrendering, being conquered, acting powerless, losing face and pride. Being gentle doesn't seem to help us become stronger, more self-sufficient, better able to cope. At best, gentleness is for somebody else to cultivate.

Although we dutifully consider gentleness to be a Christian virtue, few of us care to pray for it. We accept the distorted nineteenth-century image of "gentle Jesus, meek and mild," believing that the countless portraits and stained-glass windows depicting a bland and docile Christ accurately reflect gentleness. Unaware of its biblical roots, we avoid discovering gentleness for ourselves or understanding the central place it could occupy in our spiritual life.

Without thinking, we hold gentleness in low esteem. Yet, when the apostle Paul listed it as one of the nine fruits of the Spirit, he meant something far removed from our contemporary image of gentleness as unreasonable sweetness, powerless passivity, and timidity. Paul used the Greek *praotēs* for gentleness, a word that the noted New Testament interpreter William Barclay called most untranslatable.[1]

*Praotēs* fairly overflows with meanings. Plato considered it "the cement of society." Aristotle defined it as the mean between being too angry and never becoming angry; the gentle person expresses anger for the right reason and duration and in the right way. It is the characteristic needed when exercising discipline (Gal. 6:1), facing opposition (2 Tim. 2:25), and opening ourselves to hearing the Word without pride (James 1:21).

On the one hand, *praotēs* has a soothing quality, exhibited by politeness, courtesy, and kindness. On the other, it's a firestorm of indignation, kindled by the wrongs and sufferings of others. No matter how difficult it is to define, *praotēs* ultimately is a grace that we feel and express in balanced, Spirit-controlled ways. As Dietrich Bonhoeffer reminds us in *The Cost of Discipleship*, gentleness is a gift freely given by God that cannot exist apart from the Giver.[2]

In using *praotēs* in his epistles, Paul continued a rich tradition, for the Hebrew word used in the Old Testament for gentleness is equally complex and multifaceted. Both speak of power and meekness, oppression and strength, being and doing. The difference between the Greek and the Hebrew is mainly a matter of emphasis. Whereas *gentleness* in the Old Testament is used primarily to describe our attitude toward God, the New Testament *praotēs* dwells on the manner in which the gentle person treats others.

Implicit in both words for gentleness is what David Watson in *Called & Committed* refers to as "the primary and sovereign work of the Spirit," glorifying Christ.[3] Public as well as private gentleness then becomes an attitude and action of the heart and mind as we grow spiritually. To walk in the life of the Spirit, to let Christ's glory reflect through us to others, we must heed the biblical call to gentleness. Our world today demands it.

## A GLOBAL VIEW

All too frequently, Old and New Testament gentleness is being replaced by physical, emotional, and environmental abuse. The dynamic balance between power and respect, strength and serving, *agape* and anger is vanishing. Personal and institutional violence have become the norm.

As I write this, forty-three official and unofficial wars are being waged on this planet. Two hundred seventy people are being killed by other human beings during every hour of each day. Uncountable others are being unjustly imprisoned, tortured, or held hostage worldwide. Approximately thirty-three thousand men, women, and children each month slip below the subsistence level, succumbing to disease, starvation, and, ultimately, death. Meanwhile, our participation in the well-documented pollution of our land, oceans, and air continues with unabated selfishness.

The numbing weight of these atrocities committed throughout our global community threatens to push us deeper into spiritual apathy, a hallmark of late-twentieth-century Western society. Beset by a sense of helplessness, we find ourselves in danger of discarding the twin principles at the heart of Christian spirituality: finding God in all things and regarding all life as a religious sacrament.

## DISCOVERING THE WAY

Four hundred years ago, Saint Ignatius Loyola in his *Spiritual Exercises* taught us how to discern God's will and presence in everyday events while actively struggling to create a just and responsible society. Today, his lessons are needed more than ever.

Our commitment to strengthening the inner life while striving to right social wrongs has weakened. Too often, we dodge difficult life issues, be they the nuclear arms race, abortion, capital punishment, apartheid, world hunger, or social and economic justice. The belief that all people of God should live and die as Christ did in the service of the world holds less and less appeal for us. We are overwhelmed with crises that affect us on every level of daily living. Transformation of ourselves and society appears more and more remote, an impractical challenge beyond the scope of our limited personal resources.

Like Jeremiah, we're tempted to cry out in disillusionment and despair, until we consider the words written in 1647 by the mystic and founder of the Society of Friends (Quakers) George Fox: "When all my hopes in them and in all men were gone, so that I had nothing outwardly to help me, nor could tell me what to do, then, O then, I heard a voice which said, 'There is one, even Christ Jesus, that can speak to thy condition.' And when I heard it, my heart did leap for joy."[4]

For the first time, Fox had experienced the power of the Spirit that Christ offers to each of us. It is the only power capable of transforming our interior and exterior worlds, of leading us back to gentleness. It draws us away from the evil characteristics and limitations of the flesh and guides us toward the fruits of the Spirit, which Bonhoeffer considered "the miraculous, the created; it is never the result of willing, but always of growth."[5]

This growth is deceptively simple. It is nothing more nor less than our yearning toward God, which begins when we exchange our material sense of existence for the radical understanding of life as fully spiritual. We join the long procession of seekers struggling to find that place where the outer world conforms to our inner awareness of Truth. We look for the meaning and purpose in our lives and that of the world, and we find ourselves following the timeless spiritual path called the Way. As Meister Eckhart, a thirteenth-century friar, stated in one of his celebrated commentaries, the Way is "existence-for-God, I say, insofar as God is the principle that gives existence, and insofar as he is the end for which man exists and lives."[6]

Existing for God permeates every aspect of our lives. "For Thou hast created us for Thyself," Saint Augustine wrote in his *Confessions,* "and our heart cannot be quieted till it may find repose in Thee."[7]

The Way becomes an arduous, never-ending process involving the known and unknown, the conscious and unconscious. There is nothing automatic about it. As is true in all growth, we must strive to meet the conditions it demands in both the attitudes we hold and the actions we take. At the same time, we cannot forget the declaration of the psalmist: "For this God is our God for ever and ever; He will be our guide even unto death" (Ps. 48:14).

We are guided, we don't direct. We follow, we don't lead. But we can't begin to follow until we've grasped the paradoxical nature of the Way. Familiarity with Jesus' statement "Whosoever shall seek to save his life shall lose it; and whosoever shall lose his life shall find it" (Luke 17:33) becomes the starting point. Examining it closely, we discover the opposing truths it holds. We must give to gain, let our very self die to preserve our life. Like François Fénelon, we slowly come to understand that the soul, "ceasing its restless self-contemplation, begins to dwell upon God instead, and by degrees forgets itself in Him."[8]

In this forgetting, though, we don't lose sight of our faults and shortcomings. Although sin and imperfection, by nature, darken the texture of our life, the Divine Light illuminates them, so that we see our pride and lack of commitment, our abusive behavior and violent conduct toward others, and know how far we must go from an old life of sin to a new, gentler one in Christ. These failures are the birththroes of our transition from the reality of self to that of the Spirit.

The ancient Chinese philosopher Wu Ming Fu articulated this spiritual birthing process clearly in these verses from his *Patterns in Jade:*

> The seed that is to grow
> must lose itself as seed;
> And they that creep
> may graduate through
> chrysalis to wings.
> Wilt thou then, O mortal,
> cling to husks which
> falsely seem to you
> the self?[9]

In this labor, the seeds of gentleness finally germinate, take root, and sprout. Throughout the Bible, similar agrarian figures of speech abound, describing our inner growth with vivid, simple imagery. The vineyard metaphor used so effectively in the fifteenth chapter of the Gospel of John best illustrates what takes place next, as we move through the four stages necessary in developing and practicing gentleness in our lives.

## THE FOUR STAGES OF GENTLENESS

True outward growth begins with the unseen work of building and spreading strong, deep roots. A silent, nearly invisible process, becoming rooted enables us to resist and, ultimately, overcome the difficulties we face daily, be they spiritual droughts, emotional desolations, or the bitter winds of adversity. In his letter to the Colossians, Paul admonished them with typical fervor to learn and relearn the lessons that lie at the heart of this first stage: "So then, just as you received Christ Jesus as Lord, continue to live in him, rooted and built up in him, strengthened in the faith" (Col. 2:6–7).

Believing in and accepting Christ, we are open to his call to gentleness. With this awareness of his command, we come to the decision to follow, seeking change through study, prayer, meditation, and worship. We have embarked on what Bonhoeffer called the "hidden work of discipleship."

The second stage in developing gentleness, grafting onto the Vine, is less obvious without some knowledge of viticulture. In the vineyards of ancient Galilee (as today) propagation is done by grafting, for neither plant nor fruit remains true to type if grown entirely from seed. Jesus' imagery in John 15:5, "I am the vine, you are the branches," holds new meaning for us.

To grow in gentleness, to approach spiritual wholeness, we must learn the ways to abide in Christ, substituting his will for our own. As the nineteenth-century Swiss theologian Frederic Louis Godet reminds us, this grafting is "a continual act by which the Christian sets aside everything which he might derive from his own wisdom, strength, merit, to draw all from Christ."[10]

Grounded in faith and submissive in will, we turn to the next stage and move from belief to action. The gardeners among us know that healthy branches are pruned for one reason alone: so that the branches may bear more fruit. By utilizing the four Spirit-given abilities of humility, mercy, healing, and giving, we similarly prepare ourselves for bearing the fruit of gentleness in greater abundance. Discovering and deploying these four gifts may be painful initially, but without them, gentleness can't exist.

In the fourth and final stage, our lives become an expression of gentleness. We now know how to use the power that comes from the Spirit, to show respect for the dignity of others, to act with freedom from faulty role, race, and sex stereotyping, and to balance legitimate anger with nonpossessive, affirmative, and unselfish love. We, and all our relationships, are clothed at last in gentleness, as the apostle Paul once commanded.

I would like to speak a word of caution here. The stages I have just outlined are in some ways as artificial a construct as removing gentleness from the other fruits of the Spirit and from the spectrum of spiritual living as a whole. From my experience, I have found that developing and practicing gentleness is a spiral rather than a linear path toward reaching Christian wholeness in our lives. We encounter different steps in each of the four stages over and over again on different levels with deeper meaning. Let me illustrate what I mean by a roundabout route.

Eleven years ago, after I had given a daylong workshop on feminism and the New Testament, an elderly woman came up to me to discuss further reading on the subject. As she was leaving, she mentioned offhandedly that I was a gentle teacher. Having been in academia for a number of years, I barely took note of the teacher label, but the adjective *gentle* disturbed me. Struggling to become more assertive, I rejected the mantle of nineteenth-century gentility I assumed the woman was draping over me.

Perhaps if I had asked her what she meant by gentle, her words would never have set in motion the process that they did. I grew from blindly discarding the concept of gentleness to realizing that I didn't know what it was. And worse yet, whatever it was, I certainly was lacking it in my life.

Later, the difficult questions came. What was this fruit of the Spirit? Where did it fit into my life, my career, my multiple roles as mother, wife, and friend? How was it part of the Way? Were there steps I could take to understand it better and express it in my relationships? With maturity, could I bring it to the whole of life?

I soon discovered that spiritual searching doesn't exist independent of the seeking and growth taking place in other areas of life. In reality, gentleness cannot be easily separated from the totality of spiritual living. It becomes but one step among many along the Way. And as fruit of the Spirit, it leads toward wholeness in our relationship with God, ourselves, and others.

In a chance remark made over a decade ago, this book had its origin. From the questions raised in my mind and heart, and through the unfolding answers given by the Spirit, it flourished. Yet, in many ways, my searching has only begun. Keenly aware of this, I ask you to keep in mind the words of Thomas à Kempis: "Let not the authority of the writer offend thee whether he be of great or small learning; but let the love of pure truth draw thee to read this."[11]

From the initial heeding of the call to the final clothing of ourselves in gentleness, this book is written with that love of pure truth. It is my hope that we, the reader and the author, grow to make this gentleness of spirit our reality.

*Note to Reader:* Although we gain a valid concept of the divine nature by entering into a personal relationship with God, our ideas of God as a Person reflect more about ourselves than they do of God. I have chosen to use the masculine form for God throughout this book for two reasons: I personally feel more comfortable with the fatherly image, and it is more compatible with the primary sources I've quoted throughout the book than nonsexist forms would be.

# I. SINKING DEEP ROOTS

You have not chosen me, but I have chosen you, and ordained you, that you should go and bring forth fruit, and that your fruit should remain; so that whatever you ask the Father in my name, he may give it to you.

—JOHN 15:16

# 1. Awareness: Hearing the Call

Gentleness is Thy work, my God, and it is the work Thou hast given me
to do.

—FRANÇOIS FÉNELON

Snow is falling outside my study window. I live in a village nestled
high in the New Mexico Rockies. Snow arrives early each autumn
and lingers long, making our mountain range for several months
of the year a frozen oasis rising above the parched desert floor. But
in the snowflakes, I see nature once more playing endless varia-
tions in design and beauty. Both the diamond pattern on the shed
rattlesnake skin that I found outside my back door last spring and
the kaleidoscopic structure of the scarlet trumpet wildflower that
I placed under my microscope this summer are repeated here in the
snowflakes landing on my window ledge today.

In such simple yet eloquent ways, I am reminded that God is
personal, revealing himself continuously in the finite. With
Thomas Lawson, a seventeenth-century schoolmaster, I know that
"His works within and His works without, even the least of plants,
preach forth the power and wisdom of the Creator."[1] Everything
becomes important. Wherever we look, we glance at God and are
reminded of his presence.

Our willingness to perceive ourselves and the universe as God's
creation is the first step we take in faith. To look away from the
human sense of person and thing, to recognize that these are of
God, is to believe. We become that "finite center of consciousness,
which is able to apprehend, and long for, Infinity."[2] And in the
unfolding workings of faith, our spiritual life begins.

We believe in God with an instinct that is more than emotion,
intellectual understanding, or rational assent. As Thomas Merton

stated, believing is an "act in which the intellect is content to know
God by *loving* Him and accepting His statements about Himself on
His own terms. Our reason can tell us nothing about God as He
actually is."[3]

In this mysterious process, our awareness of God's existence
increases. We accept the Unknown and learn understanding
through the Known, Jesus Christ. We prepare our hearts to experience God; through Christ, we are led to this experience. Believing
in the divine and human Christ, we are able "to seek, to find, to
love and to be in union with God."[4]

Union with God, what a telling phrase this is! It reminds us that
our faith must move beyond mere awareness of God to communion with him. It speaks of a personal relationship that embraces
all realms of living. "Every particular thou is a glimpse through to
the eternal Thou," wrote Martin Buber of this space where the
human spirit and divine meet.[5]

But such a meeting cannot happen, we cannot be "alive unto
God through Christ" (Rom. 6:11) without the Holy Spirit also
dwelling within us. The moment we accept the risen Son, the
moment we confess that he is our Lord who redeems us, the
moment we realize everything we need is in Christ, is that moment
when we receive the Spirit.

Repeated again and again, this faith is the foundation for Christian living. It suffuses our being, pouring Divine Light into the
darkness caused by our sins. We begin to participate in the very
nature of God. The world in which we work and live takes on a
newness. We marvel at the commonplace and wonder at the ordinary, as though seeing neighbors and homes, loved faces and
familiar places, for the first time. Our consciousness has been
changed irrevocably. Now we understand George Fox's strange
cry of delight in finding that "all things were new, and all the
creation gave another smell!"[6]

This clarity extends beyond the physical. We comprehend on a
deeper level Paul's instruction to "glorify God in your body, and
in your spirit, which are God's" (1 Cor. 6:20). Belonging to him,
we desire to become Christ-like, conforming more and more to the

image of his Son. We ask the Holy Spirit to become our Counselor, helping, guiding, revealing, and releasing the reflections of the Light within us. We reject the impulses of our nature and seek the fruits of the Spirit, those Christ-like qualities that show the Spirit's movement in our hearts and actions.

## INVITATION TO GENTLENESS

Among the fruits of the Spirit, we can find many calls to follow. Each is separate and needed, yet connected and equal. This book concerns itself with only one of these calls, that which follows the biblical command to be and act with gentleness.

This command appears in the Old and New Testament no less than twenty-three times.[7] From the Psalms and Zechariah to Matthew and Peter, gentleness is demanded of us in our conduct with God and one another. In each scriptural reference to gentleness, we are given a distinct invitation to imitate Christ and model ourselves after him. We can only hope that when we hear the call to gentleness, we understand it with the same depth and clarity as Thomas Merton did. In *New Seeds of Contemplation,* he described the call as one "from Him Who has no voice, and yet Who speaks in everything that is, and Who, most of all, speaks in the depths of our own being; for we ourselves are words of His." And as words, we are meant "to respond to Him, to answer Him, to echo Him, and even in some ways to contain Him and signify Him".[8]

God initiates gentleness. We respond. Christ calls us to gentleness. We answer. When he commands us to follow him, to accept his plans for us, to commit ourselves wholeheartedly to him, and to go the way he goes without questioning, we struggle to echo his gentleness in our attitude and behavior. With the psalmist, we long to say, "I delight to do Thy will, O my God" (Ps. 40:8).

## THE DEMANDS OF DISCIPLESHIP

Christ's call to gentleness places on us certain conditions and demands that are part of discipleship. We already have touched upon the inseparable provisions of faith and obedience necessary to become a disciple of Christ. Like Bonhoeffer, we, too, know that "only he who believes is obedient, and only he who is obedient believes," for the road to faith by necessity must pass "through obedience to the call of Jesus."[9]

What we sometimes forget is that this road is one chosen for us. "You did not choose me," Christ told his apostles emphatically. "But I chose and appointed you that you should go and bear fruit" (John 15:16). Despite his unique relationship with the Twelve, Christ meant this message for all disciples in all places for all time.

Yes, we may choose to follow or remain behind, to obey or disobey, but always with the knowledge that the initial, critical choice belongs rightly with Christ. When we move from such self-centered perspectives to God-centered ones, we begin to meet the first condition of discipleship.

At this stage, we also know of the love that is expected and demanded of us when we focus our life on God. Jesus' fiery words to the questioning lawyer cannot help but burn within us, too: "You shall love the Lord your God with all your heart, and with all your soul, and with all your mind. This is the great and first commandment. And the second is like it. You shall love your neighbor as yourself" (Matt. 22:37–39).

This love starts at the Cross. As the American theologian Reinhold Niebuhr stated in many of his writings, Christianity is a faith in revelation. Through the drama of Calvary, we understand the meaning of God's love. By sending his Son to die for our sins, by ending our alienation and reconciling us to him, God through Christ taught us love and commanded us to share it both with him and with one another. Receiving and giving of the sparks of divine love is a requisite of discipleship. Unless we can hold, without doubting, the truth of God's love and strive to express it to all we meet, we will not follow for long in Christ's footsteps.

In Genesis, we learn that Enoch, the father of Methuselah, "walked with God" during his three hundred sixty-five years of living, a fact so impressive that it's mentioned twice in four verses about him (Gen. 5:21–24). I have grown to love that expression "walked with God." It confirms that our relationship with God is neither remote nor removed from the frustrations and joys we encounter in everyday living. Walking with God is a personal daily reality built on the stepping-stones of discipleship. And one stepping-stone easily overlooked in the modern, casual approach to God is reverence.

The other half of the New Testament revelation of God's love, reverence is that which makes us ask along with the psalmist, "Who can utter the mighty doings of the Lord, or show forth all his praise?" (Ps. 106:2). Profoundly aware of our own unworthiness, we acknowledge the chasm that exists between Creator and created.

More than simple fear or awe, reverence is our response to the infinite glory of God. And it is no easy struggle to match ourselves to the profile that God gave of the reverent person: "This is the one I esteem: he who is humble and contrite in spirit, and trembles at my word" (Isa. 66:2). Contemplating God, we must learn to honor both his love and his majesty, so that with Mary we may honestly exclaim, "Holy is thy name!"

Yet it is the life, not the words, of a disciple that speaks loudest: "Let your light so shine before men, that they may see your good works and glorify your Father, which is in heaven" (Matt. 5:16). Here, Jesus reminds us that adoration without deeds is empty. We are commanded to become "doers of the Word" (James 1:22) to draw others to God. Like Saint Gregory, we must hasten to put into practice what we have heard, for commitment doesn't stop with contemplation.

It becomes our responsibility to reflect the Divine Light in our relationships at home, office, school, or church. At the same time, we remain clear that this reflection can only happen through the power that comes from Christ. We accept Paul's declaration that "it is God who works in you to will and to act according to his good purpose" (Phil. 2:13). Each moment, we balance the responsibility for our actions with our total dependence upon God.

Responsibility and dependence are difficult concepts, making balance, in this context, too abstract to grasp easily. Yet it isn't much different from the lesson I learned several years ago when

I took a "powder puff" auto mechanics course to overcome my fear of what rested beneath the hood of my car.

Each week as I faced the practice engine in the shop, I entered an alien universe where my ignorance was paramount. I wish I could say that by the end of the semester I could handily repair my car at will. But reality differed greatly from my ambitions. I did grasp the fundamentals of how an engine works, and simple tune-ups are now within my scope. But the one piece of knowledge that stayed with me through the years was the importance of maintaining the correct amount of tension on the various belts. Too loose, they slipped. Too tight, and they snapped apart. In either case, without the proper flexibility in the belts, the engine wouldn't function as it should. Similarly, we must learn to maintain the dynamic tension between responsibility and dependence in our lives, to rely upon the Spirit while fulfilling our duty to act with grace.

Any list of conditions for discipleship wouldn't be complete without service. We have only to remember Jesus' rebuke to his apostles to see the importance he placed upon the spirit of service: "Whoever would be great among you must be your servant, and whoever would be first among you must be your slave; even as the Son of man came not to be served but to serve, and to give his life as a ransom for many" (Matt. 20:26–28). As his disciples, we agree to go wherever the Spirit leads us in service, be it to devote ourselves to prayer and the ministry of the Word or to lay down our life for the sake of others.

The ways of service are innumerable. What concerns us here is the radical nature of discipleship that Christ demands through service. From the stoning of the first Christian martyr, Stephen, to the hanging of Dietrich Bonhoeffer in Nazi Germany, the fullness of costly service has been repeated in the lives and deaths of true disciples over the centuries. And each act of service can be traced back to the dramatic lesson that Jesus gave when he knelt and washed the feet of his startled apostles. "I have given you an example," he told them when he had finished, "that you also should do as I have done to you" (John 13:15).

He expects us to put aside our ambitions and privileges, to follow his example, whatever the cost. We give up all rights as disciples, placing ourselves in service to Jesus and to others. Here, in this most humble of positions, we will live and suffer, know joy and pain, according to his will. In this status-conscious age in which we're repeatedly told that our identity and prestige lie in the amount of power and control we hold over others, practicing this spirit of serving is one of the most formidable challenges that we face.

Meeting the conditions of discipleship takes time. None comes quickly or easily. Yet, we have to experience faith and obedience, love and reverence, dependence and responsibility, and, finally, the selfless spirit of service before we can develop that fruit called gentleness.

Without awareness of these demands of discipleship, we are incapable of understanding the biblical roots of Christian gentleness, its exercise and expression over time, and its application in our lives and the world today. With this awareness, we can hear Christ calling us to gentleness and respond.

# 2. Openness: Being Molded Anew

> My God, here I am all devoted to Thee. Lord, make me according to Thy heart.
>
> —BROTHER LAWRENCE

Not quite two thousand years ago, a wild seer clothed in a rough coat of camel's hair stood at a shallow ford of the River Jordan near the Wilderness of Zin. There, in a voice filled with majestic power and fury, John preached a revolutionary message of hope and change.

"Repent, for the Kingdom of heaven is at hand," the Jewish holy man proclaimed again and again to the crowds who gathered from all over Judea to hear his strange, thrilling warning. "Bear fruit that befits repentance. Even now the axe is laid to the root of the trees; every tree therefore that does not bear good fruit is cut down and thrown into the fire" (Matt. 3:8–10).

The crowds wondered at his words. What was this repentance he preached? How could they bear good fruit or dare believe the Kingdom of God was near at hand?

To John the Baptizer, the answers to these questions were clear. He would baptize with water all who came to him renouncing sin on their lips and in their hearts. A single unrepeated act, this baptism would symbolize two crucial decisions made by those who sought to be baptized: a confession of past sinfulness and a commitment to moral renewal.

The repentance that John called for was nothing less than a "complete change of mind and heart and attitude, a turning from this world to God."[1] He knew that, without repentance, we couldn't gain forgiveness. And without forgiveness, the Kingdom of God would be denied us forever.

John's stern and uncompromising call was meant to prepare the Jewish people of his day for he who came after him, baptizing with the Holy Spirit and with fire (Luke 3:16). But when Jesus came to earth, lived, and sacrificed himself through a redemptive death, that call for repentance took on a fresh urgency.

Through Christ's life, teachings, and death, we discovered that to enter the Kingdom of God we need to seek God's forgiveness of our sins, and more. We must be born anew (John 3:3) to even *see* the Kingdom and the spiritual truths to which we are now blind. Repentance then becomes a necessary prelude to the death and rebirth that Christ demands of his followers.

## THE CROSS

The central overpowering reality of our repentance is the Cross. Shrouded in mystery, the lessons of the Cross are many. Unfortunately, our understanding of them is incomplete. We can only touch upon them in our imperfect way, glimpsing just a fraction of the whole.

We have already looked upon the Cross in relation to God's love. Now, through repentance, we see it also as the culmination of his forgiveness. Through his Son's suffering, abandonment, death, and resurrection, our redemption—and that of the world, past, present, and to come—took place.

Jesus referred to his death as a baptism and then promised us that "with the baptism with which I am baptized, you will be baptized" (Mark 10:39). We, too, will know death and rebirth. Like William Law, the eighteenth-century English clergyman, we will wear the mark of Christianity, becoming "dead, that is, dead to the spirit and the temper of the world, and live a new life in the Spirit of Christ."[2]

Accepting spiritual death and rebirth in imitation of Christ, we are now willing to follow the counsel given by Thomas Merton: "Enter into the darkness of interior renunciation, strip your soul of images and let Christ form Himself in you by His Cross."[3] We know we will die, be separated, and delivered from sin. We also know we will be baptized, becoming in Bonhoeffer's unequivocal words "Christ's own possession." We will share the Cross with him in a new way of living.

A new way of living. Born anew. New Creation. New Life. The new person. From the earliest Gospels to late-twentieth-century contemplative works, countless lines have been written about this dying and rebirth with Christ. Yet our fascination is justifiable. This process is perhaps the single most critical advance along the Way. It certainly is the least visible and most difficult both to explain and to attain.

## BEING MOLDED

In Psalm 37, we read that the "meek" shall possess the land. Here, as has been done several other times in the Old Testament, *gentle* and *meek* have been translated interchangeably. The Hebrew word for both means "to be molded."[4]

This passive verb clearly states what is being done to us. We are the recipients of the action; we allow it to happen. *To be molded* places power in hands other than our own. It speaks of change through an agent outside ourselves. It's full of nuances contrary to the values of this world. It automatically turns our thinking toward weakness and lack of self-control, toward giving up power and no longer directing our own destiny.

But "being molded" becomes the only route we can take if we wish to go beyond superficial change to that total one involving mind and heart called repentance. To leave the life of the flesh and enter the one of the Spirit, to move beyond the law of sin to that of God, we first must obey the command implicit in the translation of the Hebrew word for gentle. We have to place all power and control in God's hands so that he may mold us for his own purposes.

Paul Tillich stated in *The New Being,* "We belong to the Old Creation, and the demand made upon us by Christianity is that we *also* participate in the New Creation."[5] There is no way that we can share in this change until we let God move through us at will. We cannot turn from "images of the earthly" to "images of the heavenly," to borrow Saint Bernard of Clairvaux's terms, without God practicing his workmanship in us daily.

It is written in the Book of Proverbs that "the spirit of man is a candle of the Lord" (Prov. 20:27). To be fashioned by God to reflect the Divine Light requires our openness on the deepest levels. In *The Creed of Christ,* Gerald Heard wrote that "the Light shines through those who have so let themselves be opened. It is some still, firm quality, some essence deeper than deeds, that we see in them. They see Reality, are always looking at it; there is in them a quality of entire Being."[6]

We all have met these people who open themselves to being molded. The few I have been fortunate to know hold jobs as diverse as researcher, carpenter, homemaker, and professor. But no matter how different their lifestyles and personalities, they share certain characteristics that touch all who are in their presence.

We feel their quiet, joyful acceptance of whatever life offers them each day. A firmly grounded peacefulness and a genuine caring for strangers and friends radiate from them. We sense that their actions spring from the Center, unbidden yet welcome. These gentle, open people remind me of the river for which our village is named. No meandering flatland stream, this river makes its presence felt as it winds its way through town, twisting, turning, crashing over rocks and fallen timber, lingering in deep, clear pools. I sense the wind and the workings of gravity, the rains and snowmelt that propel it down the mountainside to the plains far below. Yet I cannot see the power the river reflects, only the reflection itself.

Like the river, these people mirror the Unseen Power in the daily intercourse of their lives. In opening themselves, they also have admitted the vast oceans of human suffering and tragedy around them. We ask ourselves how they can be peaceful, know restfulness, or express compassion when they see that the fate of millions is hunger and poverty, disease and persecution. Paralysis would seem a more appropriate response for them. Yet those who truly practice this biblical root of gentleness—who open themselves to being molded into candles of the Lord—react with anything but paralysis when facing the reality of the world.

Mother Teresa of Calcutta and Bishop Desmond Tutu of South Africa are two of our contemporaries who unite openness to God with openness to the human oppression and misery surrounding them. Their responses, rooted in "images of the heavenly," force us time and again to confront our own shortcomings and recognize that too often we block rather than reflect God's will. When we let go of the illusion that we somehow are in control, we can begin to end the blocking we do through denial and avoidance. Until we put to death the false beliefs we hold about our powerfulness, we cannot walk in the openness of a new life in the Spirit.

## DAILY DEATH

Francis Schaeffer, the founder of L'Abri Fellowship in the Swiss Alps, writes in *True Spirituality* that "as Christians we died, in God's sight, with Christ when we accepted him as Savior; but there is more to it than this. There is also very much the demand that in practice we are to die daily."[7]

We are asked to die many deaths after our baptism, with each death related to the central one of self. Moment by moment, through all the petty and important happenings of daily living, we hear the basic commandments of God and judge our own values and prejudices, desires and fears against them. We see the gap between our imperfect nature and the Image in which we want to be molded. We see our self-love and pride and self-deception clearly. And we wish them dead.

This may appear to be harsh language to use about a stage that leads us through suffering to a life filled with quiet hope and joy. But we are speaking about the death of a nature alien to that of Christ.

By death, I'm not speaking of a literal elimination of self. Transformation of ungodly traits into godly, rather than loss of personality, becomes our goal. Neither am I advocating that we withdraw from the world in order to lose our self in the Infinite and Eternal. "True godliness does not turn men out of the world," said William Penn, "but enables them to live better in it and excites their endeavors to mend it."[8]

We don't expect to be transformed into new people. We do expect, however, that the way we look at ourselves will change.

We will recognize in ourselves those "desires of the lower side of human nature" that Paul listed in his letter to the Galatians: "Fornication, impurity, wantonness, idolatry, witchcraft, enmity, strife, jealousy, uncontrolled temper, selfishness, dissension, heretical division, envy, drunkenness, carousing, and all that is like these things" (Gal. 5:16–20).

In this epistle, Paul gives us a detailed summary of the evils we embrace. The advice that follows is equally specific: "I warn you, as I have warned you before, that those who do such things shall not inherit the Kingdom of God" (Gal. 5:21). The apostle couldn't have made this statement any clearer. To be in union with God, we first have to eliminate sin from our thoughts and deeds. Our daily life is to become the battleground between the desires of our old nature and that of the new. From our innermost recesses to our most outward of actions, the death of the negative will take place over and over again.

In the study of Scripture, we find that a variety of images has been applied to the dichotomy between the old creation and new. We develop an outer person and an inner one, an earthly person and the heavenly one, the enemy and friend, servant and master. The terms may differ, but not the concept behind them. With transformation, our old self isn't destroyed; it still exists, along with the need to reconcile itself with the new. We are divided, and we seek union through rebirth.

## REBIRTH

The inexplicable process of rebirth is a painful struggle taking place on three distinct levels. It is a striving for reconciliation within ourselves, with our fellow humans, and with God.

The paradox that makes repentance and death of our old state possible is identical for the rebirth that will follow. Paul Tillich expressed it most clearly: "Try to reconcile God. You will fail. This is the message: A new reality has appeared in which you *are* reconciled."[9]

We don't reconcile ourselves to God, others, or self. Instead, we must allow ourselves to be reconciled, that is, "to be molded," "to be gentle" in all our relationships. And we know this has occurred when we can say, along with the apostle Paul, "True, I am alive; but it is no longer I who live but Christ who lives in me" (Gal. 2:20).

The process of rebirth begins with our struggle to end old ways. We emerge into a new world, conscious of our new state of being. God exists, and we are willing to submit to him and let him work through us. And here, at this stage, we approach the first of several pitfalls. We mistake "being molded" or "gentle" with passivity. We figure—wrongly—that all we have to do is sit and wait for God to begin to lead us toward growth.

In reality, we make the choice for God to work through us, and we actively appeal to him to take us over. We accept Jesus as our Savior. We open ourselves to receive the power of the Holy Spirit. Yes, we appear passive; actually, we are passively active. We prepare ourselves for rebirth and a right relationship with God, ourselves, and others through specific steps of our own free will. We stake everything on our growing certainty of God. We make the decision to depend not on ourselves or on our human efforts, but on divine grace. We move with utter trust and faith.

We are not unlike a Benedictine novice. When he enters the monastery, the clothing that he wore in the world hangs in his cell during his first, probationary year. He is free at any time to take off his monk's habit, dress in his former clothes, and rejoin the world. For this one year he can make the choice to enter the Benedictine order or leave without question, to move forward in his new life or return to the old. He has only to heed Jesus' warning to count the cost before he makes his decision.

In less dramatic ways, we, too, are as passively active as the fledgling monk. We enter our new life recognizing rebirth as only a beginning. We must then decide if we are to take the next step: to empty ourselves to nothingness and learn forgetfulness of self.

Over the centuries, mystical writers have struggled with descriptions of this emptying out to nothingness. For me, no explanation can match in simplicity and clarity that given by Meister Eckhart. "See an analogy in nature," he tells us:

If I want to write on a wax tablet, it doesn't matter how fine the words may be that are written on the tablet, they will still hinder me from writing on it. If I really want to write something, I must first erase and eliminate everything that is already there; and the tablet is never so good for me to write on as when there is nothing on it at all. In the same way, if God is to write on my heart . . . everything that can be called this or that must come out of my heart, and in that way my heart will have won detachment. And so God can work upon it . . . according to his highest will.[10]

Becoming detached is a rigorous process. Our perspective must change so that our sense of self is not the center and focus of our thoughts and actions. Forgetting our self requires that we negate values and attitudes absorbed from the world around us over most of our lifetime. We begin to look inward, not for reasons of self-centeredness or egotism, but to become Other-oriented. We actively desire that our life no longer be dominated by sinful human nature but by the Spirit of God.

Each step we take in self-forgetfulness is accompanied by a corresponding increase in our knowledge of God. We become empty so that God may take his rightful place in the center of our universe and of our self. We realize now that God is continually in us and around us, ready to occupy our heart.

Reconciliation with God has begun. No longer deceiving ourselves about our role in relation to God, we freely admit that he is Creator and we the created. By faith, we believe his promise that Christ is in communion with us. We know it is true when we feel a Power not our own within us. Our sense of Reality is involuntarily heightened; our sense of self voluntarily diminished.

As the facades erected by self to the world are torn away, we also see others differently. We are reminded again that for reconciliation to be complete, it must be threefold. It must happen with others as well as with God and within ourselves.

In being reconciled to others, we turn to Jesus as our teacher, for his life was a perfect fusion of theory and practice, insight and action. He translated emotion into behavior, going out among the people and living what he preached. He didn't seek final unity with the Father or Holy Spirit alone, in isolation. Instead, he gave himself to others in the ultimate example of pure self-forgetfulness.

We cannot make our relationship with God right by cutting ourselves off from other people. Daily, we must remind ourselves that we "are one body in Christ, and members one of another" (Rom. 12:5). In *New Seeds of Contemplation,* Thomas Merton drew a frightfully accurate picture of the world devoid of reconciliation between ourselves and our fellow humans. He began by stating that throughout history, Christ has suffered dismemberment, physically by Pilate and the Pharisees, spiritually by the divisions and disunity among people. "Murder, massacres, revolution, hatred, the slaughter and torture of the bodies and souls of men, the destruction of cities by fire, the starvation of millions, the annihilation of populations and finally the cosmic inhumanity of atomic war: Christ is massacred in His members, torn limb from limb; God is murdered in men."[11]

This does not have to happen. And it won't, if we stop thinking we can live our life for ourselves and by ourselves. Conversely, we have another trap to avoid here. In placing ourselves in God's hands to do as he wills with us, we mustn't think we have nothing to do with the direction that our life or the world takes. True reconciliation can come about only through being passively active. In short, we must return to the biblical root of gentleness found in Psalm 37. We must learn, moment by moment, how best to relate to God, ourselves, and others. And to do this, we must practice gentleness, which begins with being molded anew by God.

# 3. Devotion: Exploring the Kingdom of God Within

The basic response of the soul to the Light is internal adoration and joy, thanksgiving and worship, self-surrender and listening.

—THOMAS KELLY

To grow spiritually in gentleness, we next will consider the command found in the Letter of James to receive and study the gospel with gentleness (James 1:21). In this epistle dealing with Christ's ethical teachings, we come across yet another translation of *praotēs*. James, a Hellenistic Christian writing toward the end of the first century, admonished his readers with the use of *praotēs* to "be teachable" and "not too proud to learn."[1]

To become teachable and learn the Good News without pride is a logical step for us to take, for it continues the lesson of passive activity that we discovered in the last chapter. We have begun to understand what it means to be molded by God. We have emptied ourselves and engaged in detachment from the dangers of self-centeredness. Now we are ready to learn specific ways to let God fill our life with his presence.

A twofold process, this learning of God reaches both inward and outward. Here in this chapter, we will concentrate on the interior methods of devotion, including those habits of the mind and heart that bring God more fully into our life. In the next chapter, we will explore corporate methods of knowing God better through the practices of the community of faith.

## SEARCHING WITHIN

In Jeremiah's letter to the exiles in Babylon, the prophet faithfully repeated the words of the Lord: "And you seek me and find me, when you seek me with all your heart" (Jer. 29:13). He said nothing about where to seek and find. It is in Christ's declaration in the New Testament that we are given the surprising answer: "Neither shall they say, Lo here! or Lo there! for, behold, the Kingdom of God is within you" (Luke 17:21).

How simple, how obvious, how totally revolutionary to look inward to discover what Thomas Kelly called the "more subterranean sanctuary of the soul, where the Light Within never fades, but burns, a perpetual Flame, where the wells of living water of divine revelation rise up continuously, day by day and hour by hour, steady and transfiguring."[2] Through his deeply personal sharing in *A Testament of Devotion,* Kelly gives us less a manual of devotional techniques than a beautifully written glimpse into the living heart of devotion. I would strongly recommend the reading and rereading of this book as a starting point in our turning inward to know God, for few books can give us a better introduction to discovering the presence of God.

Too often we need such an aid. We tend to overlook Paul's statement to the Corinthians that we are temples of the living God (1 Cor. 6:16). That he lives in us and moves among us should make our searching for him an easy matter. Instead, we forget that recognizing, reaching out, and relating to God can happen simply by turning our attention inward.

"Let us seek God within us," the Archbishop of Cambrai, François Fénelon, wrote two centuries ago, "and we shall find him without fail." The problem is that many times we don't know where or how to begin seeking within. Again, Fénelon's wisdom can guide us: "We only need to have a heart and to desire the good . . . for true devotion . . . is all in the depths of the heart."[3]

To touch the depths of our hearts, to try to know Who dwells within, we must prepare ourselves carefully in certain timeless ways. We may find it helpful to consider the Kingdom of God as a seed in the hearts of all men and women, ready "to be produced, or rather exhibited . . . as it receives depth, is nourished, and not choked."[4] How we choose to nourish this seed, what environment we prepare for its growth, will determine how well we heed the call to *praotēs* and learn of God without pride.

As I've mentioned before, I live on a mountain high above the desert. But within an hour's drive of my home, I can move through five distinct life zones, beginning with the Artic-Alpine at twelve thousand feet down to the Sonoran at thirty-five hundred. Each zone is made up of plant and animal communities that reflect the relationship between climate and altitude. For each thousand-foot descent from the mountain to the desert below, the temperature drop is equal to a two-hundred-mile journey southward.

Within a fifty-mile radius of my house, I can walk the tundra above timberline and the shifting white gypsum sand dunes of the high desert, wade through lush, knee-high buffalo grass and orchards thick with apple, peach, and cherry trees. The lack or abundance of rainfall and the thinness or richness of air determine whether I'll see pikas or porcupines, scorpions or skunks.

The effect of temperature, moisture, and altitude upon the delicate balance of the ecosystem is dramatic and profound. With unexpected rain, the drab spring desert and summer alpine meadows turn into fields of riotous color. With a severe winter of deep snows and biting cold, the ranks of mule deer on the mountain and pronghorn antelope on the high plains thin drastically. And tomato seeds planted in the rich bottomland of the valley far below me grow to twice the height and give triple the size fruit of those planted in my yard at seven thousand feet.

Similarly, the spiritual environment we provide causes our ability to communicate with God to flower or to become stunted. Our relationship with him depends upon our creating the atmosphere in which this communication will flourish. And creating a sound spiritual atmosphere is possible when we become teachable on increasingly deeper levels. In the physical world, a delicate balance exists that must be maintained for continued growth. In our spiritual life, we must establish a similar balance between passivity and activeness, so that we may continue to learn of God without pride.

We prepare ourselves by actively raising our hearts to God, and then, in passive trust, we let God's hands hold us. Reaching within to the Kingdom of God, we finally recognize that God is actually seeking us. We are ready to learn more, not because we choose to, but because God chooses that we do. We prepare the soil for the seeds of knowledge to flourish, and we nurture them through daily practice. But we are conscious always that our growth in learning, in developing *praotēs,* happens not by our workings but by God's.

## PREPARING OURSELVES

We need to establish favorable conditions so that we may practice what Thomas Kelly called "the secret habits of unceasing orientation of the deeps of our beings about the Inward Light."[5] No such orientation can take place without our willingness to share all of our self with God.

We are trying to enter into a relationship with God, and as is true with any relationship, we must bring a vulnerable openness to it. We cannot partition off from him certain of our frustrations or disappointments, our happy plans for the evening or our schedule for the work week ahead. We are our ideas and thoughts, hopes, ambitions, feelings, and dreams. To begin a relationship and allow it to deepen, each of these aspects of our life must not be hidden, but be ready to be presented to God.

This open sense of sharing is another way of saying that we truly trust God. We are not afraid to rely upon him. We do so willingly, with no hidden secrets. With such trust, we till the soil of our soul for devotion.

By necessity, our preparations are a solitary endeavor. As we start to develop a devotional life, we experience the need to be alone and to be silent. When we choose to fill our life with the distractions of the world, we find that we cannot turn within. We feel the world pulling us away from God, and we fight it. Ringing phones, blaring televisions and stereo headsets become so much electronic interference on our channel to God. Similarly, the noise and confusion of crowded places block our access to him.

Like the Fathers of the desert, those fourth-century hermits who withdrew to the wilderness and sandy wastes of the Middle East to live in solitude, we, too, can withdraw permanently to isolated places where we can be alone and know utter silence. But we would do well to heed Henri Nouwen's advice in his excellent book on the spiritual life *Reaching Out:* "The solitude that really counts is the solitude of heart; it is an inner quality or attitude that does not depend on physical isolation."[6]

This solitude of heart goes beyond the domain of the withdrawn monk, hermit, or recluse. It acknowledges the importance of carving out time and space in our busy life to be alone and silent, to wait with a receptive attitude upon God. But it also recognizes that this isn't always possible. The noise and confusion of the world crowd in upon us when we least expect it. Work and social demands crop up with regularity, filling the moments we had reserved for quietness. But such interruptions need not stop us. We can wait upon God and be still, know a re-creating aloneness and a deep inner silence while in the thick of daily living.

Few have conducted a richer inward life while busy with worldly affairs than an obscure lay brother who worked in the kitchens of a Carmelite monastery in Paris during the mid-1600s. Known simply as Brother Lawrence, this man desired only communion with God, and he strove to accomplish it every moment he lived. "The time of business does not with me differ from the time of prayer," he said, "and in the noise and clatter of my kitchen, while several persons are at the same time calling for different things, I possess God in as great tranquility as if I were upon my knees at the blessed sacrament."[7]

We can relate to God during the crowded moments of our life and the withdrawn ones, too. We can "wait upon God in that which is pure, and stand still in it,"[8] as George Fox urged in one of his epistles to the early Quakers. And we can also learn to be "perpetually bowed in worship, while we are very busy in the world of daily affairs,"[9] as a more contemporary Quaker, Thomas Kelly, recommended. Whether alone or in a crowd, whether we are bombarded by noise or its absence, we can prepare ourselves for devotion by stepping back mentally from our surroundings and quieting our thoughts and feelings, our minds and hearts. Only in this way can we begin to free our souls to relate to God.

The opening line of one of the magnificent thanksgiving psalms teaches us how to prepare for communicating wih God. "I waited patiently for the Lord," the psalmist declared. Yet his next statements hold even greater wisdom:

> He inclined to me, and heard my cry;
> He drew me up from the desolate pit,
> out of the miry bog,
> and set my feet upon a rock,
> making my steps secure.
> He put a new song in my mouth,
> a song of praise to our God.
>
> (Ps. 40:1–3)

The psalmist had waited with patience and quieted his heart. He had cried out and was heard. He had approached God with a receptive attitude, and he had heard God in return. We, too, must learn to listen when God speaks to us. Our relationship with him is a personal one; listening plays a critical role. Throughout Scripture and the contemplative writings of those who spent their lives practicing the presence of God, we find a single message repeated again and again.[10]

Keep an open mind, and listen to the still small voice of God that I am sure speaks to thy inner self.

*Hannah Whitall Smith*

My Lord, You have heard the cry of my heart because it was You who cried out within my heart.

*Thomas Merton*

Listen rather less to your own thoughts, so as to be able to listen more to God.

*François Fénelon*

The silence of the Christian is a listening silence.

*Dietrich Bonhoeffer*

And there came a voice out of the cloud saying, This is my Son, my Chosen, listen to him!

*Luke 9:35*

From biblical authors to present-day seekers, the message remains the same. We each have the ability to hear God's voice. It isn't a grace given only to the holy prophets of old, culminating with John the Baptist. Open our minds, wait expectantly for him, be still in the recesses of our hearts, know the aloneness of spiritual solitude, listen, and we, too, will be ready to hear his voice.

## READING

On my writing desk, I keep a delicate silver woman's pocket watch. Handmade by a French craftsman sometime in the last two decades of the seventeenth century, it keeps time with amazing precision. But its central place on my desk has little to do with accurate timekeeping. Its steady, soft ticking is a gentle reminder of François Fénelon and the role this seventeenth-century abbé has played in my life.

This pocket watch was made during the years Fénelon was rising in power and wisdom within the French government and church. From leading a female community of Nouvelle Catholiques in Paris to becoming the preceptor, or spiritual teacher, of the young Duke of Burgundy, heir to the throne of France, Fénelon grew both in his relationship with Christ and in worldly influence. His fall from political and religious favor at the turn of the century through a conflict with the brilliant and more powerful cleric Bousset became one of the major events in French church history.

In his new life in disgrace in a poor diocese far removed from the court at Versailles, Fénelon penned letters "generally conceded to be the most perfect of their kind to be found in the French language. Many a believer has found solace and benefit in his thoughtful correspondence. They are, truly, *spiritual* letters and some of the best Christian correspondence dealing with the matter of a deeper walk with Christ which has ever found its way to print."[11]

High praise, and accurate when Fénelon's writings are examined. For many years I have pored over his words, delighting in his common sense, humility, simple communication with God, and profound understanding of men and women. Across three centuries, his advice and guidance have helped me enter into a deeper, richer, and truer relationship with God.

It was with a shock of recognition that I read of Thomas Merton's similar feelings about Saint John of the Cross. Merton wrote that John "not only makes himself accessible to us, but does much more; he makes us accessible to ourselves by opening our hearts to God within their own depths."[12] Much later, I found the proper term for these accessible saints who have such influence in our lives. They are a modern form of the medieval spiritual director.

Arising out of the monastic Catholic tradition, a spiritual director "must be a nurse, no more," wrote Dom John Chapman in his *Spiritual Letters* at the turn of the century. "He should confine himself to the task of teaching his penitent how to walk alone and unaided."[13]

The spiritual director, as mentor and teacher, waits upon God, listens to understand God's voice, and then guides the soul to wait, listen, and understand for itself. As an instrument of divine guidance, the spiritual director leads us to God through instruction and example in every aspect of our life. Yet, the spiritual director need not be a living person with whom we meet daily, although such a relationship is highly recommended. We may have directors in our spiritual life who are long dead but whose words remain alive to us through their writings and life stories.

The most authoritative example of this can be found in the life and teachings of Jesus Christ recorded in the four Gospels. As David Watson stated, "Jesus is God's supreme revelation of himself to man, understandable by everyone of every age and culture."[14]

Although Jesus can direct us better than any human, all Scripture gives divine guidance, God-breathed and God-spoken through the Old and New Testament writers alike (2 Tim. 3:16). In the pages of the Bible, we may hear the voice of the Director over and over again, telling us specific ways we may experience what we have read devotionally and have studied.

God also speaks to us in ways other than Scripture. His guiding hand can be felt in the devotional classics, touching our heart through the words of the writers. Our reading of devotional material oftentimes reflects our own personality, needs, and longings. Since devotional reading and study nourishes our spiritual life, we would do well to follow Dom Chapman's counsel to read only what appeals to us, recognizing that different books are necessary at different times in the soul's progress.

I approach recommending specific devotional material beyond the Bible with temerity, realizing how individual and incomplete such a list must be. I can only name those men and women who have given me varying degrees of inspiration and guidance over the last twenty years, and then encourage you to discover these and other masters who have shared their methods of meeting with God. My list begins with Augustine and Thomas à Kempis, Teresa of Avila and Ignatius of Loyola. I hold dear Saint John of the Cross, Benedict, Bernard of Clairvaux, and Francis of Assisi. I marvel at Francis de Sales, George Fox, John Wesley, Martin Luther, and Dietrich Bonhoeffer. And I consider François Fénelon, William Law, Thomas Kelly, and Thomas Merton old friends.

The list goes on. I admire the simplicity of Brother Lawrence, the clarity of John Woolman, the brilliance of Rufus Jones, and the wisdom of Meister Eckhart. Richard Foster, David Watson, Morton Kelsey, C. S. Lewis, Evelyn Underhill, Andrew Murray, Henri Nouwen, and Francis Schaeffer round out, but by no means end, the naming of those who have helped me at one stage or another in my search for an authentic spiritual life of my own. Although some have guided me better than others, to each I feel gratitude for lighting the Way.

## RECOLLECTING

A second approach to communicating with God involves recollection. If we look at the Latin root word, we find that *recollection* originally meant more than remembering. It was "a gathering in again" or, more precisely, "a gathering together."

In relating to God, recollection refers to a spiritual gathering together of our awareness and attention to concentrate exclusively on him. Of recollection, Thomas Merton wrote: "It gathers up all the love of our soul, raises it above the created and temporal things, and directs it all to God in Himself and in His will."[15]

A voluntary act, recollection can be practiced in everything we do. We begin by striving for a single perspective, that of possessing one reality, God, in our life. Seeking and communicating with God becomes central to other thoughts and actions. It dominates and influences all that we think and do.

We can find a near perfect expression of recollection in the Shaker communities that flourished during the nineteenth century from Maine to Kentucky. It was the single driving force that powered their lives. "Hands to work and hearts to God," counseled their charismatic founder, Mother Ann Lee, and her followers lived this advice, which demanded recollection at its fullest. In the process, they created enduring works of beauty. Shaker barns and homes, stairwells and chairs—even the common clothespin, which they invented—are noteworthy today for their uncluttered lines and almost flawless craftsmanship. The Shakers had learned the secret of recollected action, of working only for God and trusting that their work would reflect the One who was the sole focus of their thoughts.

The record of the Shakers' lives and work reminds us that "there is a way of life so hid with Christ in God that in the midst of the day's business, one is inwardly lifting brief prayers, short ejaculations of praise, subdued whispers of adoration and of tender love to the Beyond that is within."[16]

We, too, can learn to raise our hearts to God and push aside the distractions that move us away from him. We can kindle a more constant desire to be with God and not allow the upsets, conflicts, and problems we encounter each day to come between God and us. And, like the Shakers, we can use the power recollection develops to move us deeper into our union with God.

## MEDITATING

Meditation arises naturally out of recollection. In concentrating upon God, we have opened the channel so that we can hear clearly the still, small voice of God speaking within us. We are ready to encounter God directly now and speak with him ourselves, to break down the barriers between conscious self and the Light Within.

Both a practice and an art, meditation is another way we listen to God and learn to respond to him also. Our rational mind moves beyond reason; our faith is propelled beyond feelings. We meet God on a new level that reaches past the rational or emotional. We are in the spiritual realm where the soul recognizes its Creator. Here, God alone can give us, in Thomas Merton's words, "the sudden gift of awareness, an awakening to the Real within all that is real."[17]

By quieting our innermost self and thirsting to be touched by God, we become aware of the Infinite in a spiritual world far removed from the physical, finite one. Separating ourselves from this reality, we seek to know Another. We practice the emptying of our self, the forgetting of self, the detachment from this world and everything in it, so that we may fill ourselves with a new Self, become attached to him and what he wants us to do for him in this world.

The goal of meditation is a closer awareness and realization of God. If this sounds impractical, don't be deceived. Meditation is a discipline that is infused with practicality. Turning to Merton again, we find that people who practice meditation will "acquire the agility and freedom of mind that will help them to find light and warmth and ideas and love for God everywhere they go and in all that they do."[18] Listening to God in the silence of meditation, we will receive insight, guidance, redirection, and new effectiveness in living our lives. God establishes a relationship with us, and out of that relationship comes the impetus and power necessary for inner renewal and social change.

There is no lack of books on the techniques and methods of meditation. I have found Morton Kelsey's *The Other Side of Silence* to be one of the most comprehensive contemporary guides to Christian meditation. For those who wish to study classic methods of training, I suggest *The Spiritual Exercises of Saint Ignatius* and Francis de Sales's *Introduction to the Devout Life*.

Yet, with these recommendations I feel a word of warning is necessary. No doubt aids to meditation are helpful and needed, but we must remember that they are only jumping-off points for the spirit to prepare for the encounter with God. They cannot make the encounter happen. We must let God do it for us.

Margaret Fell, the woman who has been called the mother of Quakerism, expressed this caution far better than I. In her journal she confided that when she first heard George Fox preach, certain of his words struck her deeply: "You will say, Christ saith this, and the apostles say this; *but what canst thou say?* Art thou a Child of Light and hast walked in the Light, and what thou speakest is it inwardly from God?"

Margaret Fell next tells her reaction to Fox's question: "This opened me so that it cut me to the heart; and then I saw clearly we were all wrong. So I set me down in my pew again and cried bitterly. And I cried in my spirit to the Lord, 'We are all thieves, we are all thieves, we have taken the Scriptures in words and know nothing of them in ourselves.' "[19]

In meditation, we discover the divine answer to "What canst thou say?" within ourselves. It is the rare ecstasy felt in the light of union with God and the anguish that comes with the darkness that, at times, takes over our souls. It is blind faith and reason, pain and joy, confusion, hope, and growing awareness. We can read techniques and follow methods given by others, for they point us in the proper direction. Yet the truest way to learn and practice meditation is simply to open ourselves to God and ask to experience him.

## DEVELOPING A PRAYER LIFE

If recollection is a gathering in and meditation a reaching beyond, prayer is a life filled with Something found. It is a God-given state beyond the learned activities we follow in recollection and in meditation. In these two earlier stages, we aspire, trust, crave, and open ourselves to the spiritual realm within us. Feeling a touching of the divine, we hunger for communication with questions heard and answers received.

At times we go beyond the formulas and repetitions of given words and images. Although there is a place in every life for these traditional prayers, we now find ourselves yearning for something deeper than the deliberate and momentary. We seek a continuous and instinctive state of unworded prayer. We wish to live in what Thomas Kelly called that "inner world of splendor within" where the "real business of life is determined."[20]

We soon discover that we cannot pray one way and live another. "We learn to pray, not that one's prayer be made easier, but that one's desire for Him be made deeper, not that one can have the gifts one has not earned, but rather, the power to serve Him through each day in every tiny act," Elizabeth Hunter wrote. "We learn that everything we do it insignificant if it points toward ourselves, but strangely significant if it points toward God."[21]

It took Brother Lawrence twelve years of practicing inward prayer before he felt the presence of God throughout each day and even into the night during sleep. Like Thomas Kelly, he had learned the art of staying in touch with the listening center of life called inward prayer. He was also in touch with all that grows from this form of prayer. There is a lifetime of learning to be found in the gentle brother's example:

O my God, since Thou art with me, and I must now, in obedience to Thy commands, apply my mind to these outward things, I beseech Thee to grant me the grace to continue in Thy presence; and to this end do Thou prosper me with Thy assistance, receive all my works, and possess all my affections.[22]

Brother Lawrence's words uncover the paradox we meet head-on when trying to develop a life of unceasing prayer. We can receive such a continuous state only as a gift; yet without persistent practice, we will never achieve it. Although we need to practice turning inward to speak directly with God, although we need to discipline our self to focus the different layers of our thoughts and actions on God, our life will not become one of prayer until we receive the gift of grace to turn and concentrate upon God. Trusting is critical here, and as we learn to trust on ever deeper levels, we encounter a second paradox.

We pursue prayer and are granted it by God. We know joy; we know peace; and in the newness of centering on God, we hear him with a clarity that makes us want to sing aloud in adoration and praise. We *feel* his presence . . . and then he is gone. We are confused, heartsick, lost. We wonder what we have done wrong. In abandoning our self to God, we suddenly know abandonment. We lift our voice with the psalmist and cry:

> My God, my God, why hast thou forsaken me?
> Why are thou so far from helping me,
> from the words of my groaning?
> O my God, I cry by day, but thou
> dost not answer; and by night,
> but find no rest.
>
> (Ps. 22:1–2)

With shock, we hear the same cry echoed at the ninth hour upon Calvary. "My God, my God," Jesus called to his Father with his dying breath, "Why hast thou forsaken me?" (Mark 15:34). And the truth hits us with an almost physical force. In developing a life of prayer, we will inevitably experience spiritual desolation and dryness. Feeling deserted by God, we will know this awful yawning emptiness created by his absence. We will plunge into Saint John of the Cross's celebrated "dark night of the soul." As we discover the mystery that lies at the heart of a life of prayer, our faith and trust will be tried as never before. In the darkness of these pain-filled times, we cannot see, but we must trust, that God is drawing us nearer to him. As Richard Foster advises in his insightful book *The Celebration of Discipline:* "The dark night is one of the ways God brings us to a hush, a stillness, so that He may work an inner transformation upon the soul."[23]

A life of prayer ultimately is a life of change. "Teach me to pray," François Fénelon entreated God. "Pray Thyself in me."[24] In this manner, the life of prayer becomes the opening through which the Spirit transforms us into the image of Christ. And God, through us, begins to touch the lives of all we meet.

# 4. Belonging: Going Where Gentleness Is

The one really adequate instrument for learning about God is the whole Christian community, waiting for Him together.

—C. S. LEWIS

We have discovered the biblical commands to be and act with gentleness. Hearing these commands, we have examined three nearly invisible roots of gentleness: becoming a disciple, being molded, and learning without pride. Each of these roots grew from the husk of the seed called *praotēs*. But this seed of gentleness cannot grow into a sturdy vine without the stabilizing support of one last root: learning of God through life in a community of Christians.

The first thing we need to do is to understand what is meant by Christian community. We have read or heard of Nouwen's "community of faith," Kelly's "Blessed Community" and "Holy Fellowship," Bonhoeffer's "Visible Community," Paul's Family of God, and the biblical *koinonia* and *ekklesia*. Though the terms have differed over time and cultures, what they represent has not. The Christian community is a gathering together of God's people who have been called out *(ekklesia)* by him to belong one to another and, most importantly, to belong together in him. It is a divinely called community of belonging, where we as fellow seekers listen to hear the voice of God and act together.

This community of belonging has little to do with religious organizations, buildings, formal institutions, or hierarchies. Time, death, and distance rarely affect it. From the New Testament letter writers to twentieth-century mystics, the community of belonging has been described primarily in terms of relationships. The Body of Christ, brothers and sisters in Christ, precious members of Jesus

Christ, the one Body of all the elect, all One Christ are only a few of the phrases used over the last two thousand years to express our relationship with others through him. The community of faith came into being for the sake of these relationships, is based on relationships, and continues to exist because of relationships.

Many years ago in a speech at Pendle Hill, a Quaker study center in Pennsylvania, Howard Brinton vividly described the relationships that exist within the Christian community by comparing them to a wagon wheel of old. If we consider Christ to be the center and each of us the spokes, we can clearly see our interconnectedness with both the divine Center and one another. We soon learn that we cannot live a spiritual life alone. Although we need moments of solitude to speak to God privately, we need a community of other men and women striving to live centered lives far more.

When we take a look at first-century Christians, we understand better why this is so. These early followers of Jesus lived his command to share their lives together, with him and with one another. They heard his prayer to his Father and sought to reflect his will: "Holy Father, keep them in thy name, which thou hast given me, that they may be one, even as we are one" (John 17:11). And again: "I do not pray for these only, but also for those who shall believe in me through their word, that they may all be one; even as thou, Father, art in me, and I in thee, that they also may be one in us" (John 17:20–22).

Although our knowledge of God remains incomplete in this life, we can learn more of God when we combine private prayer with corporate worship. Without the sharing that is inherent in a true community of Christ, our growth becomes stunted and our learning eventually comes to a halt. As C. S. Lewis reminds us in *Mere Christianity:* "God can show Himself as He really is only to real men. And that means not simply to men who are individually good, but to men who are united together in a body, loving one another, helping one another, showing Him to one another. For that is what God meant humanity to be like; like players in one band, or organs in one body."[1]

## HARMONY

The first lesson we learn in seeking to join the Christian community is that of harmony. Being part of a whole moves us beyond the superficial and solitary. Taking Christ as our model, we learn by his life what is meant by belonging to his community. We realize that we must come to community with the same attitude that we have in trying to live a life of private prayer. We drop our masks and let others see us as we truly are. We are willing to be vulnerable in our openness and to share.

But in today's community, we have strayed far from the reality of the first-century Christians. We are seldom asked to give anything except on the most superficial level. We don't share every aspect of our life with others, whether it be our money, housing, food, clothing, time, energy, emotions, or work. Neither can we say: "All who believed were together, and had all things in common" (Acts 2:44). Our gatherings for worship and business, our sharing of possessions and self, rarely continue "daily with one accord . . . with gladness and singleness of heart" (Acts 2:46).

Although we may belong to churches, religious committees, prayer groups, and Bible study classes, too often we remove ourselves from deeper communion with one another. We settle for casual acquaintanceships, working friendships, or mere sociability rather than dare to develop the love that Christ demanded we show one another. We have lost that single-minded focus lived by the first disciples with their commitment to Christ and one another. We forget that "Christianity is not merely a doctrine or a system of beliefs; it is Christ living in us and uniting men to one another in His own Life and unity."[2] We need constant reminding of what it is to be part of God's family.

It means "unconditional availability to and unlimited liability for the other brothers and sisters—emotionally, financially and spiritually."[3] It means openness, vulnerability, sharing, and, above all else, unity. The forms and rituals we choose in worshiping are not important so long as we are united with God. Richard Foster warns us of this very thing: "We can use all the right techniques and methods, we can have the best possible liturgy, but we have not worshiped the Lord until Spirit touches spirit."[4]

Unity in worship consists of more than our being rightly connected with the Spirit. We lose our sense of separation from God and feel, on the deepest level possible, that we are one with him. And this union, this oneness, extends to include our fellow worshipers.

The eighteenth-century Quaker John Woolman not only wrote of unity, he lived it in such an exemplary life that it has been said, "One Woolman in a hundred, one Woolman in a *thousand,* might be enough to change the face of the earth."[5] Instead of chronicling his life and achievements, let us read in Woolman's own words the principle that guided his worship, his relationship with God and people, his life:

There is a principle which is pure, placed in the human mind, which in different places and ages hath had different names, it is however pure and proceeds from God. It is deep and inward, confined to no forms of religion nor excluded from any, where the heart stands in perfect sincerity. In whomsoever this takes root and grows, of what nation soever, they become brethren, in the best sense of the expression.[6]

Woolman believed that this inward principle, which moves us to love God, also urges us to love even the least of his creatures. Living this principle, we lose our separateness from others. Our sense of being different, perhaps of being better or worse than our fellow worshipers, our co-workers, our neighbors or friends, disappears along with our competitiveness. We become more like those spokes of the old wagon wheel. In drawing nearer to God at the center, we also draw nearer to one another.

Harmony isn't confined to church or meetinghouse, retreats, prayer circles, and study groups. Becoming C. S. Lewis's "players in one band," we can carry our worship, and the divine and human unity that comes with it, into the kitchen, as did Brother Lawrence, or into the stinking steerage of a ship traveling across the Atlantic, as did John Woolman. The classroom, bedroom, boardroom, or stockroom need not be considered off-limits here.

The early Quakers had a lovely practice that they referred to as "opportunities." They occur with less frequency today, and I cherish the memories of the "opportunities" I was fortunate enough to experience. They can best be described as the Spirit moving through a group that hasn't met expressly for worship. Whether in the midst of a business meeting or a social gathering, the group senses from one person or another a desire to grow silent and listen to the prompting of the Spirit. Gradually, all present become silent, although no words have been spoken urging this. One person may turn a prayer of the heart into words that merge with the thoughts and expressions of others in the group. The silence between words draws the group even more tightly together, before the "opportunity" fades and more typical conversation resumes. When these "opportunities" spring up unbidden and are free to happen, each member comes away with a new and often surprising sense of closeness, respect, and understanding for others within the group. Refreshed by this unexpected movement of the Spirit, we see the world and our connection with God and our fellow humans within it from a perspective bordering on the sacramental. We know at these moments what a life of unceasing prayer can be.

## INTERDEPENDENCE

Participation in the deep, inward fellowship that the New Testament writers called *koinonia* influences our lives in very specific ways. Through corporate worship at formal weekly services, more informal family devotions, choir practice, Bible study classes, or special prayer meetings, we learn lessons in receptivity. We find ourselves searching more for the good within our friends and neighbors and becoming less concerned with their faults. Our need to judge others diminishes as we feel the spirit of fellowship encompass us. Critical comments come less often to our lips while equally honest ones are spoken now with caring and compassion.

In this nonjudgmental give-and-take of Christian community, we not only learn a greater understanding of our fellow humans but also of ourselves. The community of belonging mirrors a faithful image of ourselves back to us. We see what we are and what we wish to become. At its best, this community can inspire and nurture us. At its least, it can invite change and growth through heartfelt prayer. Community can sustain or it can disillusion us. It can lead us closer to God or close our hearts to God and our fellow Christians. Above all else, it isn't an ideal that we must somehow realize. As Dietrich Bonhoeffer reminds us in *Life Together,* "it is rather a reality created by God in Christ in which we may participate."[7]

Of all the forms of participation, only one can be genuine: the fellowship in which we relate to one another as we truly are, not as we would like others to see us or how we would someday like to see ourselves. It is a fellowship in which we are not afraid to show our faults and shortcomings, our weaknesses and spiritual warts. We have given up self-deception and deceiving others. We are honest with others about who we are and what we want to become in Christ. We are not afraid to ask for help from God through the community to sustain us when we grow weak, to nurture us when we falter, and to heal us when we are hurt through sin.

We know we truly belong to the Christian community when we recognize and live the most important lesson of interdependence: bearing one another's burdens with love. Of the many fine descriptions of *agape,* or Christian love, I find that William Barclay's touches most closely to what I have experienced within community: "*Agape* is the spirit which says: 'No matter what any man does to me, I will never seek to do harm to him; I will never set out for revenge; I will always seek nothing but his highest good.' That is to say, Christian love, *agape,* is unconquerable benevolence, invincible good will."[8] In the genuine Christian community, we will be able to say, as Paul did to the Corinthians, "our heart lies wide open to you" (2 Cor. 6:11)—wide open with compassion and understanding to accept others as they are because of Christ within them.

Differences in race and social background, national self-interest, church affiliation, and cultural concern melt away in the heat of this wide-open love. "Time telescopes and vanishes, centuries and creeds are overleaped. The incident of death puts no boundaries to the Blessed Community, wherein men live and love and work and pray in that Life and Power which gave forth the Scriptures."9 As Thomas Kelly wrote with such clarity in his *Testament of Devotion*, the Christian community is not limited to those with whom we are in frequent personal contact. Just as the boundaries of our individual self disappear in worship, so have those of time, space, and distance. The Christian community of belonging extends beyond the temporal differences by which we live in this world. It is rooted in the eternal. We reach out to one another across all boundaries, acknowledging our need for interdependence and seeking the nurturing, healing, and sustenance to be found only in this community of life in God.

## TRANSFORMATION

We believe and act within community as though it is "shot through with Eternity," to use Thomas Kelly's apt phrase. We struggle to bear one another's burdens, knowing we will be united eternally with our brothers and sisters in Christ. We slowly move from selfishness to consideration and, finally, to love. Our perspectives change radically, and we become changed. With the power of the Spirit unleashed in corporate and private worship, we join in a community of God that leads us ever closer to living a life of prayer.

If this were the full extent of our fellowship with God and one another, it would not be enough. Belonging to the Christian community has one final lesson to teach us. This community is a source of great spiritual power beyond the inner transformation mentioned above. A community of faith can be world-changing, for its objectives embrace world change. We need only look at the example of the Christians of the first century, the Franciscans and the Jesuits, and the early Quakers and Methodists to be convinced that such outward transformation is a part of the Christian community's basis and goal.

Transformation begins with our reaching out to others and

helping them to know and want to walk with Christ together with us. We stop keeping our relationship with God to ourselves or confined within the comfortable but closed groups we belong to. We burn with a desire to let others hear Christ's message, awaken to his call, and share in this spiritual communion. Although we deplore hunger and poverty, deprivation and suffering, we still consider correcting these problems secondary to that of becoming Christ's disciples. We feel that belonging to the community of faith is the only real alternative to the competitive, destructive secular world in which we live. With David Watson, we feel that our commitment "to a pattern of corporate life based on radical biblical principles . . . will immediately challenge the moral, political, economic and social structures of the world."[10]

Challenge and change them. Unify and heal them. The roots of this transformation can be found only in the community of Christians, where gentleness, the *praotēs* of Paul and James, is developed through Christ within us and practiced daily in our relationship with God and one another.

# II. GRAFTING ONTO THE VINE

Abide in me, and I in you. As the branch cannot bear fruit by itself, unless it abides in the vine, neither can you, unless you abide in me.

—JOHN 15:4

# 5. Surrender: Submitting Our Will to God

In fact, apart from complete surrender of the will, there is no traffic with God.

—MEISTER ECKHART

To grow in gentleness, to approach spiritual wholeness, we now make a radical move. Or rather, we let God move radically within us. Turning to the New Testament word for gentleness, *praotēs,* we find that it has another dimension beyond being molded and teachable.

In the command given by Christ to "learn of me; for I am gentle and lowly in heart" (Matt. 11:29), *praotēs* has been translated to mean the submission of our will to God.[1] In these words, Christ told us how he considered himself in relation to the Father and to his fellow humans. In his teachings, suffering, and death, Christ showed us how he lived his Father's will, no matter the cost.

We are to hear his words of self-denial and follow, see his life of surrender and imitate it. We are to learn from him and be gentle. We are to live the lesson he taught and submit our will. We must surrender to him, as he did to the Father. And this means we must live a life of continuous struggle to follow this command.

We don't like submission. It has an ugly, groveling connotation. Surrender, filled with images of defeat, isn't much more to our liking. Giving up our will and denying our self run counter to the popular creed of self-fulfillment prevalent today. We search and can find nothing desirable about Christ's command to be gentle.

Submitting our self-centered will to God sounds difficult, and it is. By nature, we place self first. We're conditioned to think of "me," "my need," "my wants," "my fulfillment," before all else. We name everything and everyone around us in the possessive, from houses, desks, and dogs to trees, cars, and children. Our identity becomes so wrapped up in these tangible and intangible possessions that to forget our self-seeking, our self-expression, and our self-indulgences approaches the unthinkable. We heartily dislike the sound of Archbishop Fénelon's conditions of surrender: "You must give all or nothing when God asks it. If you have not courage to give, at least let Him take."[2] We honestly don't wish to either give or be taken. We like devotion, but this radical movement of God within asks too much of us.

In being molded by God, we struggled with the abandonment of self, of creating the emptiness that God would fill. The struggle still exists, except now we are engaged in this battle on a more demanding level. Though we wish to become people of "good will, that is, those who have no will save God's, which has become theirs,"[3] we also fear the perceived loss of freedom that comes with this surrender of self-will. We know that in placing our will into the hands of God, we must be ready to do everything for him. From opening our self to love to being prepared to suffer, we realize that we cannot hold back or hesitate.

We recognize that although surrender may be painful, it need not be either tyrannical or joyless. The sacrifices we make can be made willingly if we remain undivided at our core. We must belong entirely to God, pliant in his hands, wanting only what he wants and doing only what he wants us to do. In this surrender, passions for and judgments against others can fade. Our loves, longings, heartaches, miseries, and hatreds can become less "ours" and more "God's."

As we do with all struggles, at first we falter in surrendering to the divine will. We forget Jesus' invitation, which preceded his command to learn from him. "Come to me, all who labor and are heavy laden, and I will give you rest," he promised us. "Take my yoke upon you, and learn from me; for I am gentle and lowly in heart," he then ordered, before reassuring us once again, "And you will find rest for your souls. For my yoke is easy, and my burden is light" (Matt. 11:28–30).

In this passage, Christ illumines our pathway to submission. As we move nearer and nearer to surrendering our will, we grow to understand both his command and the help he offers us. We learn that his yoke can indeed be easy and his burden light—easy and light, that is, in relation to our earlier fears of what such submission would hold for us.

We still know weariness and are overburdened. The circumstances of our outer worldly life have not changed. And yet, everything has changed. The pain, grief, suffering, abuse, injustice, poverty, and humiliation still exist in our life and in the lives of those who share the world with us. But the impact these things make on our life is different because we are different.

We perceive the harsh price that we must pay for living in this world. Yet we also feel the blessings and grace that flow from our surrender of self-will. Slowly, we dismiss the question of why this high price of suffering is demanded of us and focus on using the strength that Christ gives us to deal with our problems and heartaches.

We no longer fit the sad picture that François Fénelon drew of those who will not deny self: "They only know what religion extracts, without knowing what it offers, and they ignore the spirit of love which makes everything easy. They do not know that it leads to the highest perfection by a feeling of peace and love which sweetens all the struggle."[4]

When we see what spiritual growth offers us, we shoulder Christ's yoke without complaint and discover that our anxieties, worries, and fears are quieted, our pain and grief diminished, and our troubled heart soothed. In this mysterious process of acceptance and surrender, we give much, yet, incredibly, we receive tenfold and more in return. The sacred power we set into motion when we say and truly mean, "Not my will, but Thine, O Lord," is astonishing. It strengthens, nourishes, and encourages us. And most suprisingly, it frees us.

## LOVE

When we agree to Jesus' command to surrender our will to him, we do this in a spirit of unselfish love. In his impassioned first letter to the members of the Corinthian church, Paul closes his hymn of Christian love with these lines: "Love bears all things, believes all things, hopes all things, endures all things" (1 Cor. 13:7). The love, *agape,* of which he speaks seeks to be possessed rather than to possess, to follow Another's will rather than our own, to bear and endure his burdens rather than ours, to believe and hope wearing his yoke rather than one of our own making.

Reading this you may wonder how such self-sacrificing love can possibly be freeing. Yet we need look no further than Jesus, whose life was one of submission. For love of the Father, Jesus freely chose to surrender his own will during that terrible final struggle in the garden of Gethsemane. And in so loving God, Christ both lost his life on Calvary and gained eternal life. In this paradox central to understanding and practicing Christianity, Jesus denied his self to be in loving union with God, thereby gaining the purest freedom, which is God's alone to give. As Thomas Merton reminds us, "God, in Whom there is absolutely no shadow or possibility of evil or of sin, is infinitely free. In fact, He is Freedom."[5] And God shares this with us through Christ when we, too, submit to his will in love.

Forget external domination. Forget outside pressure or compulsion through fear. We surrender for one very simple reason: we love God. In surrendering to God and loving him, we are touched by God, who is Freedom, and share in his freedom.

Without love, our submission is incomplete and resembles bondage more than freedom. We are giving, but not with our whole mind and heart. Neither are we fully loving in deed or in truth. We are divided between God's will and our own, between his desires and ours, between divine command and those of the world. We are dead and will not live; we are lost and will not be found; we are bound and will not be free so long as we resist rather than embrace God's will.

With love, all that we do for him becomes easier. I hesitate to say easy, for I have found the counsel that Archbishop Fénelon gave to a dear friend at court to be all too true: "I know not what tomorrow will bring. God will do as seemeth Him good; and this will always be our daily bread. It is sometimes very hard and unacceptable to the digestion. But listen to God, and not to yourself; therein is true liberty."[6]

Whether we have good digestion or poor, love remains the key to surrender. Saint Augustine wrote that whatever we love outside God takes away from the amount we love God. The submission that he asks for is unconditional. At times, we may feel weighed down under his burden or chafe under his yoke. At these times, we most need to examine our mind and heart, for there, hidden deep within, we will find love divided between God and self. Heal this division by uprooting self, and his yoke becomes light once again.

## ABIDING IN CHRIST

We soon find it all but impossible to live the Christian life with only our own strength and goodness. It is through God's strength that we know courage, and through his power that we know goodness. When we realize this, surrender becomes our priority. In seeking to unite our will with God's more fully, we don't want a fixed blissful union with him, one that is filled with passivity. Surrendering to him means growth and progress. It is the freedom of moving forward with and through him, so that each of our relationships and all of our work, worship, suffering, and play reflect what he wants of us.

I have wrestled with this issue of surrender more than with any other step along the Way. Whenever I felt that I had learned the last painful lesson in submission, I faced yet another more exacting one. Although François Fénelon has guided me admirably in this forgetting of self over the years, I finally learned that the struggle for total surrender so critical to spiritual growth is never over.

Originally I feared losing the identity I had spent years trying to establish and understand. More than that, I feared a future in which I held no power or, worse yet, no control. I didn't see this stance as cowardice or lack of trust in God. Weren't my actions in many other areas of my life those of a person dedicated to doing God's will? Didn't we all keep below us safety nets made of the last vestiges of our self-will just in case God was otherwise occupied? Or so my reasoning went, until one late spring afternoon when I visited a friend who has started a small vineyard in the Rio Grande valley.

Walking in the warm May sunshine, I looked in amazement on row upon row of healthy staked budding vines growing out of the sandy desert soil. Smiling at my friend's enthusiastic talk about soil preparation and pH levels, root stocks and varietals, I spied strange notched vines with incised branches connected to the notches. At least that's how these unusual vines appeared to my untrained eye.

I soon was given my first lesson in propagation and grafting techniques. Later, when my friend left me to explore on my own, I returned to the rows of grafted vines as if drawn by a magnet. Standing there staring at them, the words of Jesus echoed through my mind: "I am the vine, you are the branches. He who abides in me, and I in him, he it is that bears much fruit, for apart from me, you can do nothing" (John 15:5).

*Abide in me, and I in him.* Christ's words rose from an echo to a roar. The distant mountains, desert valley, and vineyard disappeared as tears filled my eyes and burned my cheeks. On some elemental level, I understood as never before what God expected of me and how often I had failed him by clinging to my self-will. How like the notched stock he was, and I like the scion incised to fit into the stock perfectly. Close contact made union between stock and scion complete. But in my life, time and again, I had pulled back from close contact with God, resisting union with him when I most needed to surrender completely.

I realized that there is no such thing as half-surrender, any more than the scion could half-graft to the stock. It is an all-or-none step. But I had tried to make it something in-between. I wanted to risk only certain things in following Christ, acting sometimes according to my will and other times according to his. I wanted my surrender to be a half-measure. That afternoon in the high country desert vineyard, I finally recognized that I hadn't made my world, self, mind, heart, and soul his as I said I had.

Returning home that evening, I found this warning by Thomas Merton underlined in a copy of *Thoughts in Solitude:* "Cowardice keeps us 'double minded'—hesitating between the world and God. In this hesitation, there is no true faith—faith remains an opinion. We are never certain, because we never quite give in to the authority of an invisible God."[7] Again, tears came to my eyes. Seeing the page through blurred vision, I remembered when I had underlined those sentences many years ago, so filled with confidence that I had embraced submission at last. But, in reality, I had never fully given in to God's authority or surrendered to his will.

Since that spring evening, I've discovered that, once grafted, we develop a lifelong relationship with God that deepens in understanding and practice as it matures. Our abiding in Christ, and his abiding in us, progresses through stages of growth as surely as the scion increases once it becomes part of the stock. And seeking union on deeper and deeper levels, I have tried to make this prayer written by Saint Ignatrus of Loyola a constant one from an undivided heart:

> Take, Lord, and receive all my liberty,
>     my memory, my understanding, and my
>     entire will—
>     All that I have and call my own
> You have given it all to me.
> To you, Lord, I return it.
> Everything is yours, do with it what you will.
> Give me only your love and your grace.
> That is enough for me.[8]

## THE THREE STAGES OF SURRENDER

The apostle Peter's life is a study in the three stages of surrender. When Jesus walked along the shores of the Lake of Galilee at Capernaum and beckoned to Peter, the fisherman straightaway left his nets and followed Christ. Hearing his call, Peter gave up his home, family, and business for Christ. Asked to sail across the stormy lake, Peter obeyed. Commanded to drop his nets when fishing was poor, he again obeyed Christ's orders. Given the new name of Peter by Christ, he accepted it. From keeping the secret of Christ's identity to refusing to go away from him, Peter blindly submitted to Jesus' word.

Yet this endearing apostle with the gruff, impetuous manner had his fair share of faults. Peter's concern with being first among the apostles is a thread of self-pride running through the Gospels. Refusing to accept the fate awaiting his Master, Peter foolishly interrupted Christ when he was speaking of his sufferings to come. Again, he dared to tell Jesus what to do when he saw Christ speaking with Elijah and Moses on the mountain. And vehemently, he rejected Christ's words that he would ever deny the Son of God. Yet Peter did just that, not once but three times.

Our heart goes out to the apostle as we read how Christ looked upon him in the courtyard after his denial, causing Peter to weep bitter tears of shame and regret and humiliation. And just as we have shed such tears, we have known joy similar to Peter's when he was forgiven by Christ. We smile when we picture Peter jumping over the side of his fishing boat to wade into the shore of the Lake of Galilee to be with his resurrected Lord again. We feel Peter's sadness when Christ pointedly asked him three times if he loved him. And we understand Peter's emotions when Jesus told him that he would die a death not of his own choosing, but of God's.

In his life, Peter moved from blind faithfulness through recurring surges of self-will to a mature spiritual submission of heart and mind. To use Thomas Kelly's well-chosen phrase, Peter became a "God-blinded soul" upon meeting Christ. We, too, enter this first stage of spiritual blindness when we feel God's hands upon us and in everything we do. His enlightening power washes over us, filling us with a sense of joy and wonder. Nothing else matters but God. Like Peter, we feel we can forsake everything for him and believe that we are really abiding in Christ to the fullest measure.

This joyous stage of surrender doesn't last nearly so long as we wish. At first blinded by the Light, we later begin to take notice of the darkness surrounding us. We see that we haven't let go of self completely. Our submission is superficial. Underneath, we are not fully resigned.

Joy turns to disgust and then something more insidious. We panic in this darkness and become afraid to remain entirely in God's hands. "This is where so many holy people break down and go to pieces," Merton wrote frankly. "As soon as they reach the point where they can no longer see the way and guide themselves by their own light, they refuse to go any further."[9]

Speaking from experience, I can testify to how frightening this spiritual darkness can be. In small matters and large, we see what a short distance we have come in surrendering and how far we have left to go. Our faults loom large. We seem never to be doing anything right, and dissatisfaction with ourselves becomes total. In this second stage of darkness we find no joy or comfort in surrendering because we realize how much self-will still exists. It crops up at unexpected moments in flagrant acts of disobedience and more subtle ones of pride.

In the first stage of surrender, we paint portraits of ourselves as we would like to be, believing we are fast approaching complete submission. In the second stage, our portraits are less flattering. Self, not God, remains the subject we paint, but this time with a healthy number of imperfections showing. In the final stage, we cannot be found on the canvas. There, only vivid splashes of pure color exist. We are becoming, in the expressive Quaker term, "tender" souls, who reflect submission to the Light in our day-to-day activities. Rather than being God-blinded, our souls "become more and more able to see Truth with the eyes of God."[10]

We have confidence that God will lead us where we need to go. Accepting the good and evil that is part of the Christian life, we pray and receive the strength to face whatever we encounter, explore it, and live or die as we move through it. The courage we need to accept life or death as one condition of our surrender is a gift of grace from God. As Dietrich Bonhoeffer made clear in *The Cost of Discipleship,* his gift is costly "because it costs a man his life, and it is grace because it gives a man the only true life."[11] This same costly grace strengthens us when temptation, suffering, pain, and failure enter our life. It doesn't remove them, only the fear we associate with experiencing them. We don't try to escape the painful reality of living in this world, we go forth and embrace it fearlessly, knowing we are being "guided up to God." We strive to say, along with Brother Lawrence, that we care for nothing and fear nothing. Directing all our actions to him, we desire only one thing of God—that we not offend him.

A wise Jewish scribe named Joshua ben Sira knew of the trials we would meet in surrendering our will to God. Written two centuries before Christ's birth, his teachings are recorded in the Ecclesiasticus of the Apocrypha. Although there is much worthy reading to be found there, I am particularly fond of these verses that detail how submission ultimately depends upon the grace of God:

> My son, if you come forward to serve the Lord,
>     prepare yourself for temptation.
> Set your heart right and be steadfast,
>     and do not be hasty in time of calamity.
> Cleave to him and do not depart,
>     that you may be honored at the end of your life.
> Accept whatever is brought upon you,
>     and in changes that humble you be patient.
> For gold is tested in the fire,
>     and acceptable men in the furnace of adversity.
> Believe in him, and he will help you;
>     make your way straight, and trust in him.
>
> (Ecclus. 2:1–6)

Prepare by focusing exclusively on God. Cleave to him as we encounter adversity. Trust him in the blindness, darkness, and light of submission. Accept his gift of grace and let him make straight our way. Surrender is as simple and as hard as this.

# 6. Renunciation: Giving All Rights to God

So therefore, whoever of you does not renounce all that he has cannot become my disciple.

—LUKE 14:33

The wind was blowing hard this morning, beckoning me to join the chaos outside my study window. Giving in to the noisy invitation, I took a break from writing and climbed the trail behind my house that leads to the national forest. There, high on a ridge, the majesty of the fast-approaching storm brought me to a stop.

Gray aspens, stripped of their golden autumn leaves, bent in the stiff wind. The creaking of slender lodgepole pines punctuated the protest made by other needle-laden boughs. Clouds already had enveloped the higher peaks around me, and nearby the visible rain showers, which New Mexicans call by their Spanish name, *virgas*, stood in sharp relief against the darkening sky.

Although I had forgotten my binoculars, my eyes moved automatically to search the craggy heights to the west where our resident bald eagle family has built a series of well-camouflaged nests. But I didn't need binoculars to see them, for there they were, swooping and soaring on the wild wind currents, flying with joyous abandon. As they rode the thermals high and dropped with dizzying speed, I could sense both the freedom of their flight and the precise control it required.

As I reluctantly headed down the trail back to the house, a long-forgotten verse came to mind and kept tempo with my footsteps: "His way is in whirlwind and storm, and the clouds are the dust of his feet" (Nah. 1:3). I realized anew how thoroughly every aspect of creation is God-controlled. To consider clouds as the dust of his feet puts the world in its proper perspective. We no longer think that we direct our own destiny. With Nebuchadnezzar, we confess that "all the inhabitants of the earth are accounted as nothing; and he does according to his will in the host of heaven and among the inhabitants of the earth; and none can stay his hand or say to him, 'What doest thou?' " (Dan. 4:35).

Yet when the whirlwinds and storms of life approach, we tend to forget who is in charge. In moments of weakness, we dare to ask him not only what he is doing but why he is doing it. Feeling that our desires must count for something, we pray that he act according to our expectations and balk when he doesn't lead us where we expect to be led.

## TO BE CONTROLLED

Yes, we have tried to surrender our will to him. But too often we fail, for we have overlooked an important aspect of surrender, one that comes from the now-familiar Greek word for gentleness, *praotēs.* To live gentleness and succeed in surrendering completely to Christ, we must allow ourselves to be controlled by him. William Barclay considers *praotēs* to be the gentleness that comes with "being brought under the control that is Christ's alone to give."[1]

In learning to be controlled, we don't approach God wondering what he owes us; we seek to discover what we owe him. Neither do we demand privileges to make our life easier; we embrace demanding responsibilities instead. To let Christ work through us, to let our thoughts and actions be placed under his control, we must be willing to give all rights to God.

In a discussion of the Beatitude "Blessed are the meek *(praotēs),* for they shall inherit the earth," Dietrich Bonhoeffer clearly described the fate of those who live gentleness to the fullest and, thus, are God-controlled: "They renounce every right of their own and live for the sake of Jesus Christ. . . . They are determined to leave their rights to God alone—*non cupidi vindictae,* as the ancient Church paraphrased it. Their right is in the will of their Lord—that and no more."[2]

This renunciation is more than surrendering our will to God. We are offering him the totality of our life as well. We are saying that we are willing to sacrifice ourselves in the little and great events of the day, moment by moment, as Christ once did. With the apostle Paul, we agree that "whether we live or whether we die, we are the Lord's" (Rom. 14:8). No matter what the details of daily living may be, we will strive to renounce all our rights to God every day. In offering this sacrifice of renunciation, we wish to make the present sacred by uniting ourselves more fully with God.

But how do we go about giving all rights to God? To offer this sacrifice, to make each moment holy, we must practice abandonment to an extraordinary degree. "If a man will turn away from himself and from all created things," Meister Eckhart once preached in a sermon, "by so much will he be made one and blessed in the spark in the soul, which has never touched either time or place."[3] Saint Augustine felt similarly that "the soul has a secret entry into the divine nature when all things become nothing to it."[4]

We don't give control of our life over to God until we move our heart and mind beyond the domination of self and its connection to the things of this world. In that same sermon, Meister Eckhart also said that "the man who has annihilated himself in himself and in God and in all created things, this man has taken possession of the lowest place, and God must pour the whole of himself into this man, or else he is not God."[5] Listen to this description that Bonhoeffer gave of those who have taken possession of the lowest place:

When reproached, they hold their peace; when treated with violence, they endure it patiently; when men drive them from their presence, they yield their ground. They will not go to the law to defend their rights, or make a scene when they suffer injustice, nor do they insist on their legal rights. . . . They don't belong to this earth. Leave heaven to them, says the world in its pity, that is where they belong.[6]

Bonhoeffer's statement is unequivocal. Our renunciation must be absolute. To be controlled by God, we must go out of ourselves so thoroughly that we have no attachments to this world left.

Christ's statement on renunciation is even more startlingly clear: "Whoever does not give up everything which he possesses, cannot become my disciple" (Luke 14:33). Possessions, loved ones, good things and evil, and, above all else, the core of self must be placed under his control. We love and embrace the good, hate and reject the evil as God wishes us to. And always, as part of being controlled, we are ready to give up all, if and when he asks that of us.

As we shift the focus of our being from ourselves to God, we feel the power of Christ within and understand better the workings of his grace. We know the goodness of the inner transformation that he is directing, and we grow more content with our loss of control. In this going out of self, we realize that God lets us uncover our shortcomings, weaknesses, and sins, at a pace that causes us discomfort but not despair. "He refuses us a light too advanced for our condition," Archbishop Fénelon declared. "He does not permit us to see in our hearts what it is not yet time to eradicate from them."[7] And when he asks us to renounce something in his name, God also gives us the gifts of strength and courage to bear the sacrifice if we but ask for them.

Walking along the pathway of renunciation, we approach a series of doors that God helps us to open or close. To open the door to him, we close the one to self. Opening the door to being part of the Kingdom of God, we close the door to our rights as an individual. To open the door to willing what God wants us to will, we close the door to the values and attachments of this world. We are opening in fact, not doors, but our very self to being sensitive to God's needs, being adaptable to his wants and accepting the power of growth that comes only through him and by him and with him.

Yet renunciation is not a program of precise openings readily understood by us. We encounter and re-encounter each of these doors in our life only when God knows we have the maturity in spiritual growth to open and close them properly. As in earlier stages, renunciation is accomplished through that delicate art of passive activity, which arises in the life of prayer and shows its face in our God-controlled actions.

Renunciation thus becomes "the first movement of a liberty which escapes the boundaries of all that is finite and natural and

contingent, enters into a contract of charity with the infinite goodness of God, and then goes forth from God to reach all that He
loves."[8] Even more than surrender, renunciation is freedom, particularly the freedom to see God's control in all created things and
to act freely from that same Center of control.

## RESPONSIBILITY

Along with this freedom comes the paradoxical problem of responsibility. As we become more God-controlled, we are in closer
union with him and passively receive from him those strengths
that will nurture us as we renounce even more of our rights to God.
As the eloquent evangelist and missionary Andrew Murray wrote,
we, the grafted branch of the Vine, have "no responsibility except
to receive from the root and stem sap and nourishment."[9]

On the other hand, we do have the responsibility to act as God's
representatives in *this* world where he has placed us. Christ did not
tell us to retreat from the world, but rather to "let your light so
shine before men, that they may see your good works, and glorify
your Father which is in heaven" (Matt. 5:16). The paradox we
face, then, is that he asks us to take no responsibility and every
responsibility, to passively accept the gifts of God and actively use
them in this world.

In short, we are to assume that responsibility of Christian living
called the Cross. "The Son of God bore our flesh, he bore the
Cross, he bore our sins, thus making atonement for us," wrote
Dietrich Bonhoeffer. "In the same way, his followers are also
called upon to bear, and that is precisely what it means to be a
Christian."[10]

In accepting our crosses in life, we can do so safe in the knowledge that we gain more than we suffer. Listen to this list made by
Thomas à Kempis four centuries ago:

In the Cross is salvation; in the Cross is life; in the Cross is protection
against our enemies; in the Cross is infusion of heavenly sweetness; in the
Cross is strength of mind; in the Cross joy of spirit; in the Cross the height
of virtue; in the Cross the perfection of sanctity.[11]

If we willingly accept our responsibility to bear our God-given crosses, we find that he helps bear us in return. In knowing the darkness of suffering, we also learn the quiet joy that comes with living a responsible Christian life under God's control. But such a balance is difficult to maintain.

Instead of infusing us with heavenly sweetness, strength of mind, and joy of spirit, our crosses seem, at first, to ask too much of us. In theory, we claim a readiness to live in imitation of Christ, suffering, being rejected, and dying as he did. In reality, we fight giving all to God.

It is at such times of refusal that we meet the crosses marked specifically for us to bear. "He makes us crosses of whatever we love best," Fénelon wrote, with the wisdom of one who had struggled with renunciation. "And He turns all to bitterness," he then added with equal candor.[12]

Bearing crosses can be a bitter thing indeed, if we grow afraid of letting go. Years ago I copied a striking phrase in my journal: "and I rejoice over the falling leaves of self." I'm not sure where I heard or read it, but it has been a reminder to me over the years that with suffering comes joy. In learning to bear our crosses in this life, we resemble trees in autumn. Layer upon layer of self is stripped away in the whirlwind and storm that is God-directed. Crying out in bitter astonishment at the unexpected pain, we are left naked and defenseless before the world. Bearing our crosses becomes a bleak and joyless journey that we wish were finished.

Instead, we turn back to God and ask for his strength to renounce, not our suffering, not our pain, not a particular cross, but the tight hold we have on the leaves of self. As we let go of them and begin to "live for the sake of Jesus Christ," our suffering merges with his. In this sharing, we begin to know the terrible sacrifice that Christ made for us. Ever so slowly, our bitterness fades as we finally grasp that "He suffered, and was a Sacrifice, to make our sufferings and sacrifice of ourselves fit to be received by God."[13] In a process that I can only describe as mysterious, placing our life completely in God's hands as we bear the crosses he gives us becomes an act of adoration and praise that takes us beyond suffering to joy.

## DETACHMENT

As we read about abandoning our rights to God and embracing our responsibility to bear our God-given crosses, we may find it all disturbingly removed from the ordinary details of life. Yet it is in the crucible of daily living that we practice gentleness through renunciation.

The key to renunciation is to rid ourselves of secret attachments that keep us from giving all to him. When we look at our relationship with God, we tend only to see the offerings that we make in his name. We are blind, however, to those things that we refuse to give up: "the hidden bonds which detain us," Fénelon called them.

We have many such hidden bonds keeping us secretly tied to the self. Some have their roots in the physical aspects of our life. We may have an attachment to eating or drinking, or it may be a strong appetite of a sexual nature that places our desires before God's. We may find ourselves exercising our body not only for the fitness such efforts provide but also out of a deep-seated love of self. And although there is nothing wrong with maintaining comfort in our homes or cars or offices, if our concern for well-being overrides our concern for God, we are harboring an attachment to luxuries and the money securing them that needs severing.

On the other hand, we may take no regard for our appearance and live a physical life of obvious self-denial, feeling that we are expressing our detachment from the world at large. Unfortunately, such expressions may have more to do with self-pride than with renunciation. "Everything you love for its own sake, outside of God alone, blinds your intellect and destroys your judgment of moral values," Thomas Merton wrote. "It vitiates your choices so that you cannot clearly distinguish good from evil, and you do not truly know God's will."[14]

Our physical attachments are the easiest to discover and uproot. Yet we must search for other, more deeply hidden ones if we are to truly know God's will. Examining our relationship with others is an excellent starting point. Do we act with a sense of superiority toward friends, co-workers, family, neighbors? Or are we unnecessarily subservient toward them? Are we overconfident when understanding is called for? Or resentful when opposed? Do we become stubborn when compromise more accurately reflects God's will? Do we feel possessiveness and jealousy, forgetful that all belongs to God? And what of impatience with the shortcomings, problems, and irritating habits of others?

Each of these questions seeks to uncover attitudes and behavior that are based on self-centeredness rather than God-centeredness. In relating to our fellow humans, we sometimes ignore the path that Christ traveled. We forget that he "emptied himself, taking the form of a servant, being born in the likeness of men" (Phil. 2:7). Instead, we cling to selfish ambitions, ideas, and endeavors that lead us away from serving other men and women. All too often, we aren't willing to "bear one another's burdens, and so fulfil the law of Christ" (Gal. 6:2). We hesitate to give up those secret attachments on a social level that free us to live unselfishly. Yet it need not be so:

If the world despises one of the brethren, the Christian will love and serve him. If the world does him violence, the Christian will succor and comfort him. If the world dishonours and insults him, the Christian will sacrifice his own honour to cover his brother's shame.[15]

Dietrich Bonhoeffer lived as well as wrote these words during his final years in Nazi Germany. To love and serve, to succor and comfort, to sacrifice everything for your brothers and sisters, is to follow Christ's way. We can travel this path, too, if we learn detachment from self-righteousness and self-pride in our relationships with others.

The third and final level of detachment, the spiritual one, is, by far, the hardest to reach. Thomas Merton wondered if there were twenty people alive who were free of secret attachments to "any gifts of God, even to the highest, the most supernaturally pure of His graces."[16] He finally decided that there may be one or two!

A danger in spiritual growth develops as we renounce the materialism of the world while breaking apart the chains that bind us to self. Drawing closer to God, we begin to cling to an outward form of prayer or worship, a meditative technique or fasting. At first, it appears to be an honest effort to give everything to God. Yet, we are really substituting subtle spiritual attachments for the more obvious ones of the world that we have renounced. Searching for security rather than letting our self rest in God's hands, we use spiritual exercises to express our own willfulness.

When we throw ourselves into religious activities without having made our life one of prayer, we run into a similar danger. Our days and nights are filled with teaching or printing a newsletter, working in an outreach program or a food bank, an inner-city rehabilitation project or on lobbying efforts. We feel we are doing the Lord's work, and perhaps we are. But we will never know unless we take the time to listen to his voice and be certain we are following his promptings and not ambitious ones that start in self. We must always ask ourselves whether we are working to please God or to satisfy our own need for achieving results.

Saint Theresa warned us of another danger that we encounter when we continue to place self before God: "Let us look at our own faults, and not at other people's. We ought not to insist on everyone following in our footsteps, nor to take upon ourselves to give instructions in spirituality when, perhaps we do not even know what it is."[17] She spoke with authority, for she had stumbled into this self-set trap more than once during her lifetime. Although there is nothing wrong with desiring to share the fruits of our spiritual growth with others, there well could be something drastically wrong if we do so from a selfish desire to reform them as we feel we have been reformed. Again, we have wandered from following Christ's way. Change within ourselves and others happens only when we have let go of our will and rights to embrace God's:

Less and less conscious of themselves, they finally cease to be aware of themselves doing things, and gradually God begins to do all that they do, in them, and for them, at least in the sense that the habit of His love has become second nature to them and informs all that they do with His likeness.[18]

This is how we glorify God. This is how we best preach sermons and teach spiritual lessons. It is the way we live renunciation, not the way we tell others to live it, that draws all closer to God and to a life of gentleness.

# 7. Obedience: Yielding Our Life to God

*Yes God! Yes God! Yes, yes and always yes.*

—NICOLAS DE CUSA

Abiding in Christ is a process that forces us to move beyond surrendering our will and renouncing our rights. Grafting onto the Vine requires that we develop and practice obedience as Christ did throughout his human life. If we are serious about following the biblical commands to be gentle, we first must learn the lesson of yielding our life to God in total obedience.

Obedience to God is a rather misleading concept. So often in religious writings obedience is preceded by the word *blind,* making it seem as though we muddle about in a dark prison constructed of our own spiritual ignorance. Blind obedience also conjures up images of the mindless loyalty found in personality cults of various persuasions worldwide.

Neither picture comes close to the original meaning of obedience. Its Latin root *audire* means "to listen." In our journey of spiritual growth, to be obedient to God implies that we have learned to listen to his voice and understand his call. Obedience isn't a thoughtless reflex that we make out of ignorance or misguided cultic allegiances. It is a deliberate effort to discard our spiritual blinders so that we can be in more intimate contact with God. And God, watching us trying to make the grafting successful, helps us by shedding Divine Light into our darkness. We can now glimpse his presence and let that vision guide our life.

## PREPARATIONS

God speaks to us to lead and advise and redirect our life. We can hear his voice everywhere and in all created things, if we but listen with our heart as well as our body and mind. He speaks in passages of Scripture and devotional writings. He speaks through other people's words and actions. He speaks in the seemingly unimportant events of our life, the minutiae of ordinary living. He also speaks through the tragedies and celebrations that mark human existence from birth through love to death.

He can be heard in the physical world, too. The mountains and oceans, deserts and streams all speak with the voice of the Creator. But mainly, we hear God speaking within us, and we attune ourself to listen to him with the utmost sensitivity. We begin this process of attunement in devotion, worship, and prayer. We develop it further through submission and renunciation. In stripping to the core of self, we encounter the silence of our soul before God. And in that silence, listening and understanding becomes easier if we but learn to relax.

Although physical relaxation is important in the spiritual life, I'm speaking of the relaxation that must be cultivated from within to keep the channel of communication with God open. Thomas Kelly, in his moving essay on holy obedience, gives us the key to accomplishing this: "Don't grit your teeth and clench your fists and say, 'I will! I will!' Relax. Take hands off. Submit yourself to God. Learn to live in the passive voice—a hard saying for Americans—and let life be willed through you. For 'I will' spells not obedience."[1]

To live in the passive voice is to enter into what the English mystic Evelyn Underhill termed the "sweet calm, a gentle silence, in which the lover apprehends the presence of the Beloved: a God-given state, over which the self has little control."[2] Other mystics have called this state in which communion with God can best take place the Prayer of Quiet. I prefer to think of it as that silent time of preparation in which we resist nothing coming from God and accept everything that he says.

Obedience is more than self-forgetfulness, though. In obedience, we become entirely unresisting. It is not enough to be open to his voice and to understand it in the quiet spaces of our soul. We must do something in return. Like Hosea, we must have a willingness to follow the directions we have heard, no matter how outrageous they are.

"Go, take yourself a wife of harlotry and have children of harlotry," the Lord commanded the prophet Hosea (Hos. 112). And obediently, he married the prostitute Gomer, and she bore three children, only none of them were the prophet's. When Gomer left him for good and went back to working the streets as a prostitute again, Hosea must have felt that his humiliation was complete. But God's voice continued to speak to him. "Go again, love the woman who is beloved of a paramour and is an adulteress," Hosea was told, and he complied, this time paying a substantial amount in silver and barley to get Gomer back (Hos. 3:1).

Although Hosea's story may seem an extreme example, Scripture is filled with similar calls by God for complete and unreserved obedience. From Abraham in the Old Testament to Peter in the New, we find that those who heard God's voice and responded to it did so because they hungered to live a life committed to him moment by moment and day by day. They knew that their purpose in life was to seek a relationship with God, and they accomplished this by becoming people of prayer in obedience to his call. They then sought to praise him and succeeded by living the life of prayer that he also had ordered.

We, too, are called to such obedience. Again and again, Jesus tells those whom he chooses: "Follow me." In these two simple words, Christ demands of us a life of adherence to the Word. He obeyed the Father, and we are to do the same, giving up all, denying our self, taking up our crosses daily and walking where he leads us without doubt or question.

## SELF-CONSTRUCTED BARRIERS

Our first steps in obedience are taken when we prepare ourselves so that we may hear Christ's words: "Follow me." Too often we ignore his call after that, though. We may listen, but we don't wish to do exactly what he is ordering us to do. God's directives are too difficult or obscure to understand, we rationalize. We shouldn't act because we probably have misunderstood him, we equivocate. Certainly we don't mind hearing the commandments, but it borders on the unrealistic to expect us to live them. Take Jesus' demand to the rich young man to sell everything, we say by way of example. How can anyone possibly obey that order in late-twentieth-century America? Even more to the point, how can we be certain that Jesus wants *us* to obey an order that he gave to a young Jew two thousand years ago?

Such internal arguments can continue endlessly, reflecting the nasty habit we have of erecting barriers of disobedience. All too frequently, we allow forces of our own making to come between hearing God's voice and responding obediently to it.

Just as obedience can give us access to God, so can barriers separate us from him. In every case, these barriers spring from some aspect of self that we have not fully renounced. If our renunciation isn't complete, neither is our obedience. We are placing something or someone other than God first in our life.

We separate ourselves from God when we construct the barrier of humanism. Jesus once rebuked Peter for this very thing. When Peter refused to accept Jesus' word that he would suffer, be killed, and raised on the third day, Jesus said to Peter, "Get behind me, Satan! You are an offense to me; for you savor not the things that be of God, but those that be of men" (Matt. 16:23).

We, like Peter, allow the Evil One to lead us to speak from a purely humanistic perspective. When this happens, we hear God's voice in terms of our own selfish point of view. We're not really listening to what he's saying. Rather than praying, we're hoping that what we hear will coincide with what we prefer to do. In reading Scripture, we similarly filter God's word through the values and needs of this world. We eventually question everything and accept nothing.

Along with Dietrich Bonhoeffer, we would do well to ask: "How is such absurdity possible? What has happened that the word of Jesus can be thus degraded by this trifling, and thus left open to the mockery of the world?"[3] In our arrogance, we have placed the human before the divine. We need to strip our self of pride and put God back in his rightful place as the ultimate authority in our life.

False piety is closely related to the barrier of humanism. We read and study the Bible and devotional material. We attend religious services faithfully and even belong to prayer groups or work committees. But our mind is not bright and our heart is not burning with our love for God. We have replaced fervent searching with hypocritical devoutness. We plod through the religious exercises in our life, following the letter of the law, as the Pharisees did two thousand years ago, without ever experiencing the Holy Spirit alive within us. We cling with utter flexibility to a system of beliefs that we incorrectly label "true Christianity." In reality we are conveniently excusing ourselves from obedience on the pretext of legalism and literalism. David Watson, in his challenging book *Called & Committed,* warns us of the consequences of letting false piety come between God and us: "At worst, it degenerates into bigotry, a conviction of our total correctness, which will not consider the possibility that we are mistaken. Literalism refuses to listen to what other people are saying, and, worse, to what God himself may be saying through these people."[4] Be it the dryness of legalism or the hardness of literalism, false piety effectively blocks our communication with God.

Doubts also force themselves between God's call and our response. In doubting, we allow our self-concerned voice to drown out the truth-filled one of God. Letting our trust of God slip through our fingers, we speculate about what he could possibly mean in this scriptural statement or that. As he leads us, we falter, questioning intellectually if this is the correct direction for us to take. As always, Thomas Merton strips away all illusion with his perceptive remarks about doubting:

Fickleness and indecision are signs of self-love. If you can never make up your mind what God wills for you, but are always veering from one opinion to another, from one practice to another, from one method to another, it may be an indication that you are trying to get around God's will and do your own with a quiet conscience.[5]

Refusing to live in the present moment is yet another barrier constructed by self. Instead of focusing on the eternal, we remain firmly fixed in the temporal. Tied to time, we rush hither and yon, desperately seeking to "fill" every hour with our accomplishments. Yet, to hear God's voice, we would do better to "empty" a part of each hour and day to listen quietly to what he is saying to us. "From the first to the last moment of life, God never means us to look upon any time as purposeless, either to be used as our own apart from Him, or lost," Archbishop Fénelon counseled. "The important thing is to know how He would have us use it. . . . For remember, we lose time not only by doing nothing, or doing amiss, but also by doing things in themselves right, which yet are not what God would have us do."[6]

Many of those things we do amiss, or correctly for the wrong reasons, arise from lingering dependence upon self instead of God. Like Martha, we have our priorities upside down. Preferring busyness to listening to Jesus' words, we show by our actions that *we* know how best to use "our" time. With a crowded calendar of activities, we pay scant attention to listening to God's voice. After a while, we become so busy, we find it easier to respond to our self than to him.

Jesus gave a harsh warning to those who erect such barriers: "But he who hears and does not do them [my words] is like a man who built a house on the ground without a foundation; against which the stream broke, and immediately it fell, and the ruin of that house was great" (Luke 6:49). When the apostles asked Christ who then could be saved, he answered simply, "With men this is impossible, but with God all things are possible" (Matt. 19:26).

We can be saved from the ruin that Jesus predicted by building our foundation upon the promise he gave. By ourselves, we will achieve nothing. Through obedience to God's will, our life will become a way to the Kingdom.

## OFFSHOOTS OF OBEDIENCE

As our union with God becomes more complete through obedience, we begin to experience certain unexpected benefits. I say unexpected because when we feel their presence in our life, we also feel a jolt of surprise that we should be thus blessed by God.

Gratitude numbers first among these gracious offshoots of obedience. In becoming more God-centered, we feel a sense of thankfulness, recognizing that God in his goodness is caring for us. Only when we grow totally dependent upon him through obedience do we finally admit that everything about us is of God.

We admit it and want to give thanks. "Oh that men would praise the Lord for his goodness, and for his wonderful works to the children of men!" declared the psalmist. "So let them sacrifice the sacrifices of thanksgiving, and tell of his works with rejoicing" (Ps. 107:21–22).

In the concordance, I found over a hundred other biblical references expressing an overpowering need to show gratitude to God. From the Levites and Daniel to the psalmists and the healed leper, each felt compelled to offer thanksgiving to him.

But the gratitude we wish to express must encompass the bitter as well as the joyous in our life. Even in our suffering, we need to recognize his goodness and learn to give thanks to him for enacting in our heart "the miracle of willingness to welcome suffering and to know it for what it is—the final seal of His gracious love."[7]

Under painful circumstances and happier ones, obedience will produce heartfelt gratitude for all that we have been given, if we only live in the Spirit. It will also produce orderliness. We learn in the first chapter of the first book of the Bible that God created the earth and gave it order. So has he done with us. But for us to live in the orderliness he intended, we must obey God's basic commandment to love him above all else and love our neighbors as ourselves. Anything less, and chaos rears its ugly head in our life, confusing our thinking and behavior. When we are obedient to God's will, our life does not become more complicated and cluttered, as we might expect. Instead, we have but a single focus that orders all our thoughts and actions. It doesn't matter if it makes no sense to those of this world. Since God is Order, we trust that in following his commands we will reflect his orderliness in our life.

As God shares his orderliness with us through obedience, so does he share his peace. In much of the devotional material written about spiritual growth, we read this or similar phrases time and again: "and I was learning to be content." This contentment is not based in self but in the peacefulness that comes with placing self entirely in God's hands.

In obeying him, we are bringing to an end the conflict between the human and divine. We no longer are at odds with God, resisting him at every twist and turn along the spiritual path. In obedience, we have joined with him to live for the eternal values that alone bring contentment. We experience what Thomas Kelly called the Eternal Now with its "invariable element . . . of unspeakable and exquisite joy, peace, serene release. A new song *is put into* our mouths . . . for the Singer of all songs is singing within us. It is not we that sing; it is the Eternal Song of the Other, who sings in us, who sings unto us, and through us into the world."[8]

## ABSOLUTE OBEDIENCE

Living in the present moment but rooted in the eternal, we discover that our negative responses to our difficulties and problems disappear in proportion to the degree we obey him in each thing he asks of us. We sing a new song composed of gratitude, orderliness, and contentment, but how loudly we sing depends entirely upon how well we obey God. We must yield our lives to him, not only "with all the stretch and all the strength of our hearts, but also with all the concentration of our thoughts," to use Fénelon's colorful phrase.[9]

A full life of obedience cannot happen at once. We can start right where we are now, though, living this moment in obedience as best we can by listening sensitively, breaking down barriers, and remaining open to him. And if we forget God for a moment and listen to the discordant voice of self, we should start over again, right where we are in this present moment. With practice, moments will stretch to hours and then days so long as we continue to say no to self and yes to God.

There can be no halfway obedience, just as there is no halfway renunciation or surrender. To say to God, "yes, but," is disobedience plain and simple. When we are called to a life of obedience, that call is absolute. "He who *believes* in the Son has eternal life;

he who *does not obey* the Son shall not see life, but the wrath of God rests upon him" (John 3:36).

To believe in him is to obey. There is no other way. "If you believe, take the first step, it leads to Jesus Christ," Dietrich Bonhoeffer stated. "If you don't believe, take the first step all the same, for you are bidden to take it. No one wants to know about your faith or unbelief, your orders are to perform the act of obedience on the spot."[10]

To abide in Christ is to abide in the present moment with unconditional obedience. We don't wish to have the final word, to reinterpret God's demands in terms of our worldly needs, or challenge his message with our intellectualism, doubts, and fears. "With Jesus it is all, or nothing," David Watson declared. "To be in the Kingdom of God is to accept Jesus as King; and if he is King, his word has final authority and must be obeyed."[11] At this stage in our quest for gentleness, we acknowledge, accept, yield, and obey. We know there is no other way.

# 8. Subservience: Doing God's Will

As sure as it is our duty to look wholly unto God in our prayers, so sure is it that it is our duty to live wholly unto God in our lives.

—WILLIAM LAW

We have found that being true to the biblical command to gentleness means that we must submit our will to God, renounce our rights, and yield our life to him through obedience. Yet we cannot complete this stage of becoming gentle by abiding in Christ until we understand and practice subservience in our relationship with God and others.

Subservience is a most practical and straightforward process. Fusing being with doing, subservience is both a spiritual attitude and a worldly action. Coming from the Latin "to serve under," subservience defines our position in the spiritual life as serving under God. While being in his service, we also are charged with serving others.

A means to an end, subservience is a powerful instrument in developing gentleness to its fullest. It takes our spiritual surrender, renunciation, and obedience and brings them together in this world where we are challenged to *do* the will of God. When the apostles asked Jesus to teach them how to pray, the order of his response is as instructive as his words. After praising the Father's name and proclaiming the coming of his Kingdom, Jesus taught us the meaning of subservience: "Thy will be done on earth as it is in heaven" (Matt. 6:10), he promised the Father.

Jesus left no room for any other interpretation. First and foremost, we are to serve under God. In our life here on earth, we are to do his will in all things. And to fulfill his will, we must live both a contemplative interior life and an outward one committed to service in his name. In our subservience to God, the inner journey of recognizing God's will culminates in our actions. We hear his voice, yield to it obediently, and respond by doing what he asks of us.

Although he is the Son of God, Jesus didn't consider "equality with God a thing to be grasped, but emptied himself instead, taking the form of a servant" (Phil. 2:6-7). Christ insisted on placing himself in a subordinate position to both God and other people, and so must we. For us to be fully subservient, we are to "serve under" our fellow humans. We are to take to heart Paul's admonishment to "do nothing from selfishness or conceit, but in humility count others better than yourselves" (Phil. 2:3).

The ramifications of adopting subservience to God and to others as a way of life are far-reaching. The hierarchical structures governing relationships in society no longer are relevant. As Richard Foster explains, "Leadership is found in becoming the servant of all. Power is discovered in submission."[1] It doesn't matter whether we hold a superior or inferior position according to the culture in which we live. Once we become subservient to God, we have no choice but to become subservient to all others. That is the only position that matters.

We have prepared ourselves for this by renouncing our willfulness, our self, and all our rights attached to self. We now move forward to embrace our new subservient status in this world as we live by the rules of another—totally spiritual—one. We no longer identify ourselves by the position we hold in society. Instead, subservience governs how we perceive ourselves, how we perceive others, and how we relate to them and to God.

Martin Luther popularized the *Haustafeln,* a table of rules for the Christian household based upon the ethical instructions found in the Pauline and Petrine epistles in the New Testament. In the *Haustafeln,* wives and husbands, masters and slaves, parents and children are admonished to fulfill duties according to their earthly roles. But the instructions in the epistles don't necessarily support the prevalent social structure.

John Yoder, in his excellent scholarly study *The Politics of Jesus,* rightly argues that "the *Haustafeln* do not consecrate the existing order when they call for the acceptance of subordination by the subordinate person (wife, slave or child); far more they relativize and undercut this order by then immediately turning the imperative around."[2] Subservience, to be true, must be mutual, practiced by the persons deemed dominant as well as by the ones considered inferior by the society in which they live.

Despite the roles we may play within the family, business community, church structure, or society at large, subservience is a position that we must take if we wish to continue to grow spiritually. Jesus led a life of absolute subservience to God and to others. We are to follow along the same path, guided, as always, by his example.

## THE KEYS TO SUBSERVIENCE

There are three ways in which we must change if we are to dedicate ourselves to serving under God and our fellow humans. The most obvious and inclusive key to subservience is learning to live *in* this world but not *of* it. Placing spiritual authority above the human, we begin to interpret the actions of others in the light of God's Word, and then we respond accordingly.

Our obedience is given wholly to God-ordained authority. Although we also live in subservience to human authority, we do so only when it doesn't contradict the laws of God. The world's values and standards—meaning human values and standards—hold little power in our lives. We live in subservience to God the Father, the Son, and Holy Spirit, responding to the Voice within and the Word without.

In doing this, we can learn from the experiences of François Fénelon. When a papal commission denounced his book *The Maxim of the Saints,* the archbishop immediately recanted, in effect renouncing his own teachings. He did this out of a firm belief that he was to be submissive to the pope and to the mother church in all things.[3] And when Fénelon was then banished to a diocese far removed from everyone and everything he loved, he submitted to the spiritual authority of the pope once again. He devoted the remainder of his life to his humble parish duties while penning the letters that have guided so many seekers down through the centuries.

Fénelon hadn't sought to rebel against the pope or the Roman Catholic church, which he considered the seat of spiritual authority here on earth. He had tried to filter his thoughts and actions through the divine commission to do God's will, and when told he was wrong, he submitted.

On the other hand, the archbishop hadn't sought to rebel against human institutions and their laws either. Yet in Fénelon's life he came into direct opposition with human authority while working at the royal court of Versailles. In 1685, when King Louis XIV revoked the Edict of Nantes, persecution of Protestants under his rule increased. In this and several other instances, Fénelon chose to serve under God rather than the king, sowing the seeds for his later downfall. He went to the heavily Protestant districts of Poitou and Saintonge and ministered to "the heretics" until he was recalled to court by an exasperated king.

There will be moments in our lives, too, when we will have to make a choice about whom we will serve and be willing to accept the cost it will extract. As the German philosopher Johannes Hamel reminds us, subservience carries with it "the possibility of a spirit-driven resistance, of an appropriate disavowal and a refusal ready to accept suffering at this or that point."[4]

We learn that, in serving under God, we must refuse all destructive human orders and accept the consequences imposed upon us by the authorities in and of this world. Suffering cannot be avoided when following in Christ's footsteps. Although our minds turn automatically to the ultimate sacrifice he made and the similar one that could await us, other forms of suffering mark the subservient Christian.

Like John Woolman, we may appear "weak and foolish to that wisdom which is of the world" as we "stand in a low place, rightly exercised under the cross."[5] Or we may know the humiliation of Hosea, the heartache of Abraham, or the torments and agony of Job.

Thomas Merton gives us this disturbingly accurate description of the subservient follower of Christ:

One of the signs of a saint may well be the fact that other people do not know what to make of him. In fact, they are not sure whether he is crazy or only proud; it must at least be pride to be haunted by some individual ideal which nobody but God really comprehends. And he has inescapable difficulties in applying all the abstract norms of "perfection" to his own life. He cannot seem to make his life fit in with the books.

Sometimes his case is so bad that no monastery will keep him. He has to be dismissed, sent back to the world like Benedict Joseph Labre, who wanted to be a Trappist and a Carthusian and succeeded in neither. He finally ended up as a tramp. He died in some street in Rome.

And yet the only canonized saint, venerated by the whole Church, who has lived either as a Cisterian or a Carthusian since the Middle Ages is St. Benedict Joseph Labre.[6]

But we are not saints. Most of us live our lives within families and fellowships, neighborhoods, villages or urban communities, nations and, ultimately, that international community called the world. These groups can be divided along many lines, but to the subservient Christian the one that divides brethren from non-brethren is the clearest. And in that division, we can find the next key to subservience, reciprocity.

As Paul stated in the opening paragraphs of his letter to the strangers within the church at Rome, he shared a mutual faith with them. And through this shared faith, a reciprocal relationship had been established between them in Christ's name. In another letter to the members of a church with which he was familiar, Paul commanded the Ephesians to "be subject to one another out of reverence for Christ" (Eph. 5:21). It mattered little to Paul whether he had met his fellow Christians or not. He knew them in Christ and recognized the relationships that existed between them as fellow members of the Body of Christ.

In the early church, Paul wasn't alone in acknowledging the reciprocal nature of the Christian relationship. From the Gospel of Matthew to the Epistle of Jude, the New Testament is replete with references to the reciprocity that binds us together. Abiding in Christ, we are joined with our fellow Christians. And as branches united in the Vine, we let our relationships with our brethren reflect our subservient one with God.

We practice this reciprocity in a number of ways, which signal to the world that we serve under our brothers and sisters in Christ. It may be our willingness to listen to the troubles of a family member or friend, or the sharing of our time on a church work project. A visit to the sick, or a meal for the overburdened, house-cleaning for the overworked, and a shopping trip for the housebound all are small acts of subservience we can make daily.

In my home, we have what we've dubbed The Reciprocity Jar, which is filled with slips of paper listing our names and the jobs we heartily dislike doing around the house and yard. Sitting in full view in the kitchen, the jar gives family members the opportunity to serve one another whenever we choose to open the lid and draw out one of the unpopular jobs. In writing this, I wonder if The Freedom Jar might be a more accurate label, for the third key to subservience, freedom, is certainly at work here.

We are granted freedom when, as Christians, we no longer are of the world but are in it serving as God wills us to serve. We don't operate with our own freedom, but with what he gives us of his. And his freedom helps us serve all men and women, not just those called brethren. It doesn't matter if the reciprocity that exists in our relationships with other Christians is missing. With the grace of the Holy Spirit working within us, we are now free to touch that of God in every person through our acts of service.

It is in this freedom that the roots of servanthood flourish and spread. We are not tied to the more worldly ethic of doing to others as we would have them do to us. We have incorporated the heart of Jesus' message into our lives, believing that we should do as Jesus has done to us and what the Father has done for us by sending us his Son. The need to dominate and be in control of our relationships has disappeared. We don't serve out of a fear that if we treat others badly, we will receive the same in return. Our hearts are free to serve the downtrodden, the outcasts, the poor, despised, and helpless simply because Christ did the same:

Where the world seeks gain, the Christian will renounce it. Where the world exploits, he will dispossess himself, and where the world oppresses, he will stoop down and raise up the oppressed. If the world refuses justice, the Christian will pursue mercy, and if the world takes refuge in lies, he will open his mouth for the dumb, and bear testimony to the truth.[7]

This is how Christians who know the freedom of God act. And when we combine this freedom with a reciprocal subservience toward one another and place spiritual authority above the human, we are well on our way to doing God's will.

## THE SUBSERVIENT PERSON

I have always been drawn to the mountains. I enjoy hiking and feel happiest when I'm climbing a switchback trail above ten thousand feet. There, approaching timberline, with the trees and oxygen thinning, I see and feel the world from a changed perspective.

As I climb upward, I find that my body doesn't work as effectively as it did at lower altitudes. If I don't give myself time to adjust to the demands of this new environment, my body will show signs of mountain sickness.

Similarly, I need to give myself time to make certain mental adjustments. I am used to seeing our village, ski area, cars, lakes, and other mountain ranges from a lower elevation and a safer site than a narrow path above the treeline. Security is stripped away up there. In the wild openness, everything gauged by the human scale appears insignificant. Uphill progress has brought me to a strange and frightening place unless I shed my old perspective and embrace a new one.

While climbing, I focus on the act of getting up the trail, paying little attention to the changes taking place around or in me until I stop. But once stopped, I notice both my labored breathing and the considerable expanse now separating me from the village far below.

In our spiritual growth, we follow a similar trail. Climbing the mountain of subservience, we tend to focus so steadily upon God that we overlook the changes taking place around us and in us. We don't stop often enough to make the necessary adjustment to the demands of the changing landscape. Yet it is during these spiritual rest stops that we learn to discard the old perspective and put on the new. We see our dominating ways more clearly and how far we must go to be made completely in Christ's subservient image.

There are six qualities that the subservient Christian has, and it would be worthwhile for us to check for these during our moments of rest. We can begin by questioning whether our acts of subservience are *voluntary,* coming from a willing heart. We would do well to ask ourselves whether we remain *reverent* while striving to be faithful to God's voice. Do we feel *joy* serving under God and others? And finally are we *straightforward, loyal,* and *dependable* as we seek to do his will? It is by these six marks that our spiritual growth in subservience can be measured.

The voluntary and reverent aspects of subservience are fairly obvious. Not so with joy. When writing about three athletes of the spirit—Kagawa, Gandhi, and Schweitzer—the American minister Allan Hunter stated that if you put the three in the presence of youngsters, "in five minutes they will all by having a jolly and probably hilarious time. . . . These three have humor not because they have escaped but because they have embraced the sufferings of the underprivileged and the tasks of social change."[8]

Such joy appears paradoxical, but it isn't. It springs from our subservience to God and others, and only subservience can produce it. It is the virtue bestowed upon us when we are doing God's will, and it becomes both a privilege and a duty. Subservient Christians have every reason to be joyful and should be joyful, for they alone share in the joy of God.

If joy is the quality that makes us want to embrace subservience, integrity is the one that constantly tests our adherence to it. Compromising the truth, social lying, manipulating the facts, and exaggerating are only some of the ways in which we reject God's will. We cannot serve under him and others by being deceitful in word, thought, or action. When we fail to be honest, we also fail in being subservient. Since there is no aspect of our life in which integrity isn't an issue, we need to remain alert to how easily deception can take root and stop us from responding to God's voice obediently.

We also respond to God's voice when we act in a reliable manner with all we encounter. We keep our word or discharge our obligations, not out of convenience or personal whim, but because it is God's will that we be dependable in all things. In Psalm 15, when David asks who shall be admitted to God's temple, the answer given is only those men and women who have the requisite moral qualities, including the ability to keep an oath even when it hurts. We do not allow ourselves to be distracted from the task at hand, even if meeting that commitment proves costly to us.

None of these qualities can exist within the subservient person without loyalty. Unshakable, persevering loyalty is the keystone of subservience. Without an unswerving fidelity to the Triune God, we shall possess neither subservience nor God's presence in our life. Speaking to the young men of a Dominican community in Germany in the thirteenth century, Meister Eckhart told them that no work, whether it be great or small, could be fully achieved without loyalty: "A man's being and ground—from which his works derive their goodness—is good only when his intention is wholly directed to God."[9]

As we climb the figurative mountain range of spiritual growth, it is true that we must practice the habit of dwelling continually in the presence of God. Beyond that it seems, at times, as though there is little to do in doing the will of God; and yet, there is an enormous amount that must be accomplished. Let us listen to François Fénelon's wisdom on the complementary movement between being and doing by which we fulfill God's will:

We must never hold back anything, or resist for a moment this Divine love which searches out self-will in the most secret recesses of the soul. But, on the other hand, it is not the multitude of hard duties, it is not constraint or contention, which advances us in our Christian course. On the contrary, it is to yield our wills without restriction and without choice; to go on cheerfully from day to day as Providence leads us; to seek nothing, to refuse nothing; to find everything in the present moment; and to suffer God, Who does everything, to do His pleasure in and by us, without the slightest resistance.[10]

That is the only formula we can follow if we wish to grow in gentleness. We surrender and renounce, are obedient and subservient. God's will, not ours. His rights, not ours. Our life mirroring his Son's. Seeking nothing but God's will and finding everything in it. When we have grafted onto the Vine this completely, we know the meaning of gentleness and are now ready to put our belief in gentleness into action.

# III. PRUNING THE BRANCHES

Every branch that does bear fruit he prunes, that it may bear more fruit.

—JOHN 15:2

# 9. Humility: Joining the Poor in Spirit

> Be gentle and humble in heart, that is to say, let gentleness spring from real humility.
>
> —FRANÇOIS FÉNELON

There are many lessons to be learned from the mountain on which I live, none so expressive as the one taught by the bristlecone pine. This unusual evergreen holds the longevity record in the Rocky Mountains, living for as long as 4600 years. At lower elevations, it grows to thirty feet, but near timberline, it resembles a shrub more than a tree.

The bristlecone pine adapts in other ways, too. With age, its whitish bark turns deep reddish brown, and the trunk twists and angles with the years. To see an old bristlecone pine close to treeline is to understand the history of the local climate. Permanently bent in the direction the wind most frequently blows, its gnarled branches hovering over the sparse ground cover of the mountain's upper reaches, the bristlecone pine speaks of a marvelous resiliency as it continues to flourish under harsh conditions.

Although only a dwarf version of the giant pines below, this tree plays a complex role in the delicate plant and animal community that manages to survive near timberline and above. Its roots stabilize the poor mountain soil and provide footing for the fragile grasses, sedges, lichens, and tiny alpine flowers. This vegetation, in turn, supports marmots and pikas, ptarmigans and water pipits.

This is only the beginning of the bristlecone pine's service to this high-altitude community, but unraveling this web of interdependent relationships is a story best left for another time. Suffice it to say that the bristlecone pine survives in order to serve.

We, as Christians, similarly survive to serve. But our service is not the natural, unthinking response of the physical world. Ours is the result of gifts given to us by the Spirit so that we may be better equipped to do God's will. A means to an end, these Spirit-given abilities are bestowed upon us to benefit others, not for our individual glory. Receiving these gifts, we become instruments of God; using them, we serve him by helping others know his glory.

The list of spiritual gifts that we may receive numbers anywhere from nine to twenty-eight, depending upon the source. We will concern ourselves with only those four that are critical for developing gentleness in our lives. Much as the gardener prunes healthy branches to increase the yield, God shapes and trains us to bear the fruit of gentleness in greater abundance through the use of his gifts of humility, mercy, healing, and giving.

Like pruning, developing these four gifts may prove painful initially, but without them, orderly, God-controlled growth will be replaced by the stunted, nonproductive growth only of self. In cultivating these gifts of the Spirit, we will move through stages of active dislike and discomfort to grudging toleration and genuine enjoyment. Only gradually will we begin to understand why the Greek word for spiritual gift, *charisma,* is so closely related to the Greek word for joy, *chara.*

Looking at the first of the four gifts needed to bear the fruit of gentleness, we may find ourselves wondering how humility can bring us from pain to joy. In asking ourselves that, we're not much different from the English jurist John Selden, who antagonized the clergy three hundred years ago with his remark that "humility is a virtue all preach, none practice, and yet everybody is content to hear."[1] Another Englishman, T. S. Eliot, looked upon humility with a similarly honest eye, finding it "the most difficult of virtues to achieve; nothing dies harder than the desire to think well of oneself."[2]

## STOOPING DOWN

I'm not certain whether humility is the most difficult of all virtues to achieve, but it definitely is the hardest of these four gifts of the Spirit to exercise consistently. Perhaps it has to do with humility's relationship to gentleness. In the King James Version of Psalm 18:35, David proclaimed "Thy *gentleness* has made me great," but in the New International Version, the same verse is rendered "You *stoop down* to make me great." As Jerry Bridges (in *The Practice of Godliness*) writes about this difference in translations, gentleness takes on yet another nuance in meaning, that of "stooping down to help someone. God continually stoops down to help us, and he wants us to do the same."[3]

And the most direct way to be gentle, that is, to stoop down, is to develop and practice the gift of humility. We begin by examining the section of Paul's letter to the Romans where he warns them "not to have a mind proud beyond that which a mind should be. . . . Keep your thoughts from pride; and never refuse to be associated with humble people" (Rom. 12:3–15).

We are to know ourselves, without conceit or false modesty, exactly the way we are. Recognizing that the standards by which the world judges us aren't necessarily the same ones used by God, we learn that humility begins with thinking far less of ourselves and far more of everyone else.

The apostle Paul wasn't the only one to approach humility by coupling honest self-appraisal with how we view others. "The highest and most profitable reading is the true knowledge and despising of ourselves," Thomas à Kempis declared in *The Imitation of Christ.* "It is great wisdom and perfection to think nothing of ourselves, and to think always well and highly of others."[4]

This may seem a simple injunction to follow if we think only of those we love, admire, and respect. But what of our other brothers and sisters, those whom we barely touch in disdain or turn our backs to in outright rejection? We may not place our prideful thoughts into words, but don't we consider ourselves better, less sinful, more worthy than certain others we meet in the course of daily living? Yet, to stoop down as Christ did, we must consider ourselves *less* worthy and *more* sinful than all we encounter. Paul considered himself in this light, and so, too, did Thomas à Kempis. Our instinctive tendency is to reject these words, for they place us in the most servile of positions, as they are meant to do. Yet, without this basic attitude, no progress in humility can be made. Struggling honestly to embrace such a lowly position, we are ready to descend to the next rung on the ladder of humility.

## THE DEPTHS OF HUMILITY . . .

This next downward step involves putting a stop to the power that the world exerts over us. In our grafting onto the Vine, we have renounced being *of* this world, but our worldly renunciation is nowhere near complete. Who among us doesn't swell with pride when complimented for a job well done? What is our natural response to receiving applause, being awarded an honor, or winning a prize? And what about our reaction to an unexpected raise or bonus?

There is nothing wrong with the pleasure we feel in each of these situations, but we are a long way from humility if we receive the good fortune God grants us and neither acknowledge the Source nor thank him for it. If we consider any of the above forms of praise our just due for being hardworking good Christians, or if we secretly hold ourselves alone responsible for being thus rewarded, we don't know humility. We still care too much for the honors, advancements, and approval of this world—and too little for the One responsible for making it happen.

Similarly, when we encounter situations in our life that fill us with sadness and pain and longing, we come face-to-face with the issue of humility once again. Do we rebel at the senselessness of a young child's suffering and death? Do we rail against the unfairness of being fired from a job we performed well? Do we despair when unexpected bills wipe out our meager savings? What about our feelings when we helplessly watch disease ravage the mind and body of a beloved parent?

Such rebellious, angry, and despairing responses spring from our pride and conceit as surely as the pleasurable ones do. Our concern remains with our life in this world and not with God. We dare to place our earthly needs and wants above spiritual considerations. We presume to know what is best for us and those we love. We proudly refuse to give credit where credit is rightly due—to

God—for what we are, for what we have, and for what we encounter and accomplish, whether it be joyous or pain-filled.

Humble women and men recognize and live by the truth found
in the prophet Isaiah's words: "Thou hast wrought for us all our
works" (Isa. 26:12). The world holds no power over them. Only
God matters. "Humility is nothing else but truth," François Fénelon confided to one of his faithful correspondents. "And there
are only two truths in the world, that God is all, and the creature
is nothing. In order that humility be true, we need to give continual homage to God in our lowliness, and to stay in our place, which
is to love being nothing."[5]

If we have a high opinion of ourselves, we aren't humble. If we
take exception to the suffering God wills, we aren't humble. Neither are we humble if we seek only the pleasure and good fortune
that God also wills. Whenever we place our reputations, needs,
wants, and interests before his, we distance ourselves from humility and from God. But when we sincerely desire to put God in his
rightful place and ourselves in the one that consists of being nothing, we have moved deeper into true humility.

Desire alone is not enough to attain humility. We feel disgusted
with ourselves as we see the number of insidious ways we fail in
being humble. Clever remarks or learned quotations come back to
haunt us, as we realize that we include them in our speech and
writing for our own glory, not God's. The new car we choose to
drive, the furniture we buy to decorate the house, the clothing we
wear all are simple, functional, economical expressions of our
spiritual values. Or are they? We need to ask ourselves if we
picked out that quietly expensive sport jacket or that original oil
painting to impress others with our prosperous position in life.
Conversely, are we clinging to the attic-eclectic style of furnishing
our home or clothing our body to stress our prideful, if not false,
solidarity with the less fortunate?

"How can you be humble if you are always paying attention to
yourself?" Thomas Merton asks us. "True humility excludes self-
consciousness, but false humility intensifies our awareness of ourselves to such a point that we are crippled and can no longer make

any movement or perform any action without putting to work a whole complex mechanism of apologies and formulas of self-accusation."[6]

The next downward rung brings us past this self-conscious mind-set that ends up in apologies and self-accusations. Discouraged and disgusted with our lack of humility, we move now to lift our burden of false humility instead of stumbling beneath its weight. We begin by doing, for *humility* is an action word at heart. As a gift of the Spirit, it has one purpose, and that is to serve. And we can best attain it by serving others.

In *Life Together,* Dietrich Bonhoeffer gives us a hint how to begin. "Nobody is too good for the meanest service," he wrote, making it clear to us that any time, anywhere, and under any circumstances is the right moment to start helping others.[7]

It doesn't matter if the assistance we give is trifling or large, of short duration or long. What does matter is that in being helpful, we are following God's way and not our own. To learn humility, we must always keep God as our central and only concern. "It is part of the discipline of humility that we must not spare our hand where it can perform a service," Bonhoeffer acknowledged, before adding, "but we do not assume that our schedule is our own to manage, but allow it to be arranged by God."[8]

In following God's schedule, we have approached the bottom rung of the ladder of humility at last. We are ready to join the poor in spirit and become one with those who have entered into a holy and voluntary spiritual poverty.

In no way is this emphasis on spiritual poverty meant as a dismissal of external material poverty. Christ practiced financial poverty and commanded it of his apostles: "Get you no gold, nor silver, nor brass in your purses; nor scrip for your journey, neither two coats, nor shoes, nor staff; for the laborer is worthy of his food" (Matt. 10:9–10). Nothing was to interfere with their labor in the spiritual fields. Their outward circumstances would accurately reflect their inner commitment to be humble, to be nothing, before the Creator.

Such voluntary financial poverty eliminates the barriers we

erect in our fear of becoming totally dependent upon God. Accepting this poverty means we need God and are willing to turn to him to fulfill our needs, that we love him and, for that love, we will surrender those things that stop us from loving him fully.

Dependence, not material poverty, lies at the heart of Jesus' command to the rich young man to sell all and follow him. We must give up everything that comes between God and us. *Everything.* Even though we sell our possessions and live a life of external poverty, we still may be no closer to God, no closer to practicing humility or to living in the spirit of poverty that he demands of us.

"Blessed are the poor in spirit, for theirs is the Kingdom of Heaven" (Matt. 5:3). With these words, Christ embraced and elevated the spiritually poor, promising them his Kingdom. But who are the poor in spirit, the *ptochoi to pneumati* of Matthew's Gospel? A correct translation is "those who know their need of God."[9] Realizing their own abject helplessness, the poor in spirit rely wholly upon God. The noted historian Michael Grant described these people as those

who since they have confidence in no earthly authority or salvation but in God alone, are particularly likely to possess the right attitude of humility and repentance for securing entry to the Kingdom.[10]

This is what God wants us to become. This is what he commands us to be. "A poor man wants nothing, and knows nothing, and has nothing," Meister Eckhart preached in his famous sermon on the poor in spirit.[11] We must dare to be this poor in a world that honors materialism. We must depend fully upon God in a world that applauds rugged independence. We must serve friends and strangers alike in a world that holds such service in contempt. We must take no honor in being called poor in spirit, instead accepting this label with the utter humility it deserves.

## . . . AND THE HEIGHTS

After climbing down to the depths of humility, unburdening, discarding, and unlearning the practices of this world along the way, we next must journey upward to understand humility in its entirety. And on this journey, we encounter the first uplifting, yet paradoxical, aspect of humility.

We are serving as he arranges us to serve. We are actively discarding all vestiges of our vanity and pride. We are placing God first, and others before ourselves. We are becoming children of God, dependent upon his grace and will. We deserve nothing, expect nothing, take nothing, accept and resist nothing. We are being led where he wills, and to the world we appear sorry excuses for people.

We seem too childlike in our approach to serving others. We certainly aren't fulfilling our potential by worldly standards, for humility rates low on all scales of success except the spiritual one. We are cutting across the cultural grain. We seek subservience in a dominating society. We strive to help others when the prevailing motto is Win Through Intimidation. We number ourselves least when others scramble for the top position. We have embraced the desire for an absolute lack of power and control in our life.

Now listen to this ancient story of a desert father, Abba Macarius. One day as he was on his way back to his cell from the marsh carrying a heavy load of palm leaves he had cut, the good abba met the devil along the way. The devil was holding a sickle with which he had planned to beat Abba Macarius, but, to his surprise, he found that he couldn't make himself hit the defenseless old man.

"I suffer a great deal of violence from you, Macarius," the devil cried out in frustration. "I do everything you do. When you fast, I do not eat. And when you keep vigil, I don't go to sleep at all. Yet there is one thing in which you outdo me."

"And what is that?" Abba Macarius asked.

"It is your humility," the devil replied. "And because of it, I am powerless against you."[12]

As we explore humility, we discover that the powerlessness perceived by those of this world is, in reality, a reflection of the power of God. Christ exemplified humility from the beginning of his earthly life in a stable to the end of it on a wooden cross.

Through his humility, we can glimpse into the heart of God and know his power. "Perfect humility implies perfect confidence in the power of God, before Whom no other power has any meaning and for Whom there is no such thing as an obstacle," Thomas Merton said in *New Seeds of Contemplation.* [13] In going to the depths of humility, we know total powerlessness, and in climbing toward the heights of humility, we recognize the greatest Power.

We now experience the second by product of humility, freedom. When we have stripped ourselves to nothingness, expecting nothing for ourselves and everything from God, we no longer are imprisoned by our fears and doubts and anxieties. We are bowed down in service. Yet, instead of feeling miserable in our existence, we know the joy of being liberated. Our acts of service, which bring us ever closer to humility, aren't limiting. We are free to help the sick and impoverished, the weak and less fortunate, the hurting and the needy. Everyone becomes our neighbor, the cruel and despotic as well as the kindly and democratic. Our hands can produce so much more now that our hearts are free.

We also have the freedom to rise above the pain of our service and that given by the world for having served. There is another story told of the desert fathers, this one about Abba Poemen:

"If a monk overcomes two things," the good abba stated, "then he can be free from this world."

"And what are they?" another brother asked.

"Bodily ease and vainglory." [14]

We overcome bodily ease with voluntary material poverty and eliminate vainglory with poverty of the spirit. Together, they add up to a life lived in humility through service at its deepest and its highest.

# 10. Mercy: Shouldering the Cheerful Burden

> If the occasion arises when we must show mercy, let us do so with gracious cheerfulness.
>
> —ROMANS 12:8

Humility is elusive. The more we try to embrace it, the quicker it is to recede. Not so with mercy, the second serving gift of the Spirit that helps us develop gentleness. Mercy is both simple and direct. With no difficulty at all, we can define the compassionate nature of mercy, recognize it when we see others living it, and know how and when to use it ourselves.

In its simplicity and directness, mercy appears to be a gift we use instinctively, rising effortlessly out of our desire to become more Christ-like in all our relationships. Having none of the dark, mortifying aspects of humility, mercy apparently flourishes in the cheerful light of love. All we must do is show practical compassion to whomever needs it. That's all!

It's at this point that we should step closer and examine mercy from a new perspective. Shortly after I first moved to New Mexico, I visited a Navajo weaver on a nearby reservation. Like many Eastern transplants, I soon grew to love the intricately designed weavings and longed to learn more about their history and symbolism as well as the mathematical precision of the techniques that transform random strands of sheep wool into these stunning works of art. Over the years, I've been fortunate enough to indulge this interest with books and firsthand experience. Time and again, when I see my clumsy attempts at weaving or look at the truly masterful ones of Native American weavers, I think of the gift of mercy. Let me explain.

To casual observers, these Indian weavings appear beautiful or eye-catching or merely interesting in their harmony, color, balance, and design. We may notice size, shape, or texture, appreciate the overall artistic effect, or sense the ancient roots of this craft. But the weaver, and the careful observer, can see each work with a different eye, one that considers each strand individually and understands why its placement, color, shape, and thickness is true to the pattern being created.

When we look at mercy, we tend to be like casual observers. We see the gift of mercy as a whole without bothering to examine the individual strands that together create it. We see that mercy is showing practical compassion to the needy. We know that joyousness can come from doing deeds of loving kindness and that suffering can be alleviated when our caring turns into genuine acts of sharing. Yet, to find out what mercy consists of, we must consider its various intertwining strands and seek to understand what they are and why they are needed in creating this gift of the Spirit.

## FORGIVENESS

Forgiveness is woven tightly into the fabric of mercy. In fact, without forgiveness, mercy cannot exist. Before we are able to feel compassion for others and to work to alleviate their suffering, we must recognize God's unconditional forgiveness of our sins and adopt that same attitude toward those who have wronged us. This twofold process of forgiveness comprises the second petition found in the Lord's Prayer: "And forgive us our debts as we forgive our debtors." Not only must we approach God with a contrite heart and candidly admit our wrongdoing, but we must also forgive others who have hurt us. We cannot, in good conscience, ask our Father to forgive us when we have failed to forgive others. These two attitudes are forever linked together spiritually. One cannot exist without the other.

When he taught the Lord's Prayer and the parables of the unmerciful servant, the prodigal son, and the sinner at Simon's house, Christ made it abundantly clear that when we seek forgiveness, we become reconciled with God. He doesn't turn a deaf ear to us in a gesture of lingering ill will or resentment. Nor does he lash out in retaliation for the pain we have caused him to suffer. Instead, God embraces all who turn toward him with an honest request for forgiveness on their lips and in their hearts. His forgiveness ends our estrangement, making it possible for us to enter into a richer, closer relationship with him.

But we must always remember both parts of the petition in the Lord's Prayer. How can we expect God to show an unconditional loving readiness to forgive when we hesitate to do the same to others? In these ten words, "And forgive us our debts as we forgive our debtors," Christ has given us the key to deepening our relationship with God and with others. We must be willing and able to forgive others as we wish to be forgiven. If we cannot or will not, we need to find out why and correct our unforgiving attitude. Using this petition as a practical guide to daily Christian living, we realize that we won't be reconciled with the Father so long as we insist on harboring old hatreds and hostilities toward our fellow human beings.

Through this prayer, Christ avoided a superficial approach to divine and human relationships. He demanded that we probe the painful bitterness, animosity, and antagonism of our daily encounters. Seeing how these negative feelings darken our life, he asked that we place such spite and ill will in the light of his experience and let go of them.

Yet, we will never be able to let go and turn to our brothers and sisters in a spirit of loving forgiveness until we cut out the remnants of self-pride that prevent us from forgiving others. For it is pride that makes us remember the hurts and scorn we have received. It is also pride that allows the insults and undeserved rebukes we have endured to fester within.

This destructive pride rooted in self is the diametric opposite of what Christ taught us on Calvary. There, he demonstrated his total selflessness. He took on our sins, antagonisms, pride, and resentments, and then sacrificed himself on our behalf. He forgave us our faults and brought us back to the Father. Even as he was being nailed to the cross, Christ prayed this unselfish prayer of unconditional forgiveness: "Father, forgive them, for they know not what they do" (Luke 23:24). He experienced God's forgiveness and extended forgiveness, unasked, even to those who were killing him. Should we do any less in our own lives?

"Nothing greater can happen to a human being than that he is forgiven," Paul Tillich wrote in *The New Being*. "For forgiveness means reconciliation in spite of estrangement; it means reunion in spite of hostility; it means acceptance of those who are unacceptable, and it means reception of those who are rejected."[1] Reconciliation. Reunion. Acceptance. Reception. We gain these four things when we are forgiven by God, and we share them when we learn to forgive others.

## FORBEARANCE

A wonderful quality with an old-fashioned ring to it, forbearance is the second crucial component needed to practice mercy. At first glance, forbearance appears to be one and the same thing as forgiveness. Upon closer scrutiny, we find that though forgiveness implies a heartfelt pardoning of those who have wronged us, forbearance suggests something more far-reaching.

As Paul used the word *forbearance* in his letters to the churches in Asia Minor, he meant it as a bearing with the faults of others in a spirit of loving tolerance. With forbearance, we look beyond forgiving our debtors. We now need to learn how to accept and tolerate everyone we encounter, complete with their failings, annoying habits, and irritating mannerisms.

To express the gift of mercy, we first have to rise above our finding fault with others. We leave little room for compassion if we fill our thoughts and conversations with comments on the weaknesses and failures we perceive in other people. I dare say we spend a great deal of our energy discussing others' stupidities, incompetence, and bad habits. And when we're through with these less-than-charitable topics, we're apt to focus upon the poor unknown driver ahead of us who moves too slowly through traffic or the neighbor who cuts the lawn at seven in the morning or the doctor who keeps us waiting an hour for our appointment.

I may appear unduly harsh in this discussion of our lack of forbearance. Yet an experiment I took part in a few weeks ago attests to the fact that we—and I include myself in this observation—simply don't practice bearing with the faults and failings of others. This experiment began innocently enough. Lingering over coffee in a local restaurant, a group of friends and I were discussing forbearance and agreed to pay close attention to the number of times during that one day we heard or made unkind remarks about others, voiced criticisms of their shortcomings, or showed impatience with their ways. Since we live in a resort village with a daily influx of tourists from neighboring states and cities, we thought our informal poll, although small, would accurately reflect Southwestern behavior.

The results surprised and discouraged us. Not a half hour had passed without someone giving vent to frustration about the faults of another person. Whether going about a workday or a vacation, tourist and townsperson alike showed a remarkable lack of forbearance.

I don't think we can excuse our actions by saying that the stressful complexities of life in twentieth-century America make bearing with one another impossible. Different as they were, daily interactions were similarly difficult for the Ephesians of the first century. More than once, the apostle Paul had to beg them to lead lives worthy of being called Christian through "lowliness and meekness, with patience, forbearing one another in love" (Eph. 4:2). No matter how much progress we seem to have made over the centuries, showing each other loving tolerance remains a challenge, one that we must meet if we want to utilize the gift of mercy.

## SILENCE

Silence is a natural outgrowth of forbearance. In learning to tolerate others, we refrain from commenting on their habits and behavior in a negative and destructive manner. We hear these words of the psalmist and take them to heart:

> You give your mouth free rein for evil,
>> and your tongue frames deceit.
> You sit and speak against your brother;
>> you slander your own mother's son.
> These things you have done and I have been
>> silent; you thought that I was one
>> like yourself.
> But now I rebuke you, and lay the charge
>> before you.

(Ps. 50:19–20)

Silence in mercy means more than stilling our tongues whenever we plan to speak evil. We must silence our judgmental thoughts as well. Each time we think of another person critically, we need to consciously isolate that thought and replace it with one that is imbued with gracious tolerance for his or her faults. As Dietrich Bonhoeffer discovered, the person who practices this ministry of silence "will be able to cease from constantly scrutinizing the other person, judging him, condemning him, putting him in his particular place where he can gain ascendancy over him and thus doing violence to him as a person."[2]

In such silence, we allow others to exist as God made them to be rather than how we would wish them to be. Whether they be cruel or kind, inept or competent, dishonest or just, irreverent or devout, it isn't our place to judge and condemn others for not conforming to that image that we assume is godly.

Through the use of silence, we not only drive out our desire to dominate and control but also learn to listen to one another. When we truly hear what others are saying to us in the respectful silence of our heart, we can begin to serve our fellow humans with mercy, for we now know what they need from us and can respond accordingly.

## CONFRONTATION

A 180-degree turn from silence, confrontation appears to be an unusual choice to include in the fabric of mercy. Yet, it does add a necessary and vibrant color to this gift of the Spirit. Forgiving others, tolerating their faults, and silencing our judgmental tongues and hearts are merciful responses to make in certain situations. But there are also times when we can show mercy best by confronting another person about a bad habit, a slight or hurt, a hidden resentment or failing.

Again, we look to Jesus as our teacher and learn from him that confrontation as a component of mercy begins by having the right attitude. Before we dare to remove the speck of dust in our brother's eye, we first must dislodge the log in our own. Are we seeking confrontation out of a deeply rooted concern for the other person's welfare? Or are we confronting him or her out of impatience, irritation, or stubborn pridefulness? Are we approaching the discussion with love for the other person? Or are we filled with criticism and disdain for him or her? It is important that we correct with love, as Paul once reminded the Ephesians. But we must also be careful that our correction "is good for edifying, as fits the occasion, that it may impart grace to those who hear" (Eph. 4:29).

Jesus corrected the apostles on several occasions, each time balancing his love with the need to open their eyes to their failings and shortcomings. In his parables, too, he confronted those who would not or could not hear his message directly, and he forcefully reproved them to change their ways.

Whenever he was moved with compassion, Jesus expressed that caring in acts of mercy. Making the blind see and the lame walk, he confronted those who dared to criticize him for acting thus. In more cases than not, Jesus then went on to point out his critics' faults, always coupling that with an invitation to follow him.

His apostles didn't shy away from confrontations that carried concern and love for the other person along with the correction. Look at Peter's reply to Simon of Samaria when the misguided disciple tried to buy the power of the Holy Spirit. Although Peter dealt harshly with Simon's deception, he acted more tenderly toward the deceiver: "Repent therefore of this wickedness of yours, and pray to the Lord that, if possible, the intent of your heart may be forgiven you. For I see that you are in the gall of bitterness and in the bond of iniquity" (Acts 8:22–23).

Mercy needs the cutting edge of confrontation, for this aspect brings about change in a most effective manner. Without confrontation, mercy is merely a patient, forgiving, tolerant reaction to the shortcomings and failings of others. With confrontation, it is all of the above and something more. We, through the Holy Spirit, are capable now of creating change in the person we confront, leading him or her closer to God by our attitude during the confrontation. Mercy, with the strands of confrontation woven through it, moves us deeper into the realm of service, where all gifts of the Spirit rightly belong.

Service through confrontation in today's world, was graphically illustrated in a recent editorial cartoon. In it, we see an arrested nun who works for the sanctuary movement asking a judge, "What is the charge, Your Honor?" Leaning over the bench, the judge responds, "Mercy, with intent to embarrass."[3] Embarrass, perhaps. Confront and serve, most definitely.

## DISCIPLINE

Any examination of mercy would be incomplete without considering the practical role that discipline plays. Simply put, we need to practice forgiveness, forbearance, silence, and confrontation whenever the proper occasion arises. The more frequently we exercise these four aspects of mercy, the easier it will become for us to feel compassion for the needy and to do something constructive with that compassion.

Discipline transforms. "Exercising itself, virtue grows strong, and in its generosity it becomes mighty," Meister Eckhart lectured in his treatise on divine consolation.[4] We need look no further than the life of Elizabeth Fry to see the truth of his statement.

A nineteenth-century Englishwoman and mother of eight, Elizabeth Fry, by her own account, was consumed by the knowledge that she had been given the gift of mercy in order to serve. "Since my heart was touched at seventeen years old, I believe I never have awakened from sleep, in sickness or in health, by day or by night, without my first waking thought being how best I might serve my Lord," Elizabeth told one of her daughters.[5]

But it wasn't until Elizabeth was thirty-three years old that she discovered how best to serve him. Visiting Newgate Prison for the first time at the suggestion of an American Quaker activist, she was appalled by the conditions she found there. Seeing the filth, noise, and degradation the imprisoned suffered, Elizabeth could have chosen to ignore them and return to her comfortable and loving household.

Instead, she decided to fight for prison reform, and she succeeded beyond all expectations. Male prisoners were separated from the women, hardened criminals from first and minor offenders. But Elizabeth Fry wasn't satisfied with these rather impressive results. She next fought for more sanitary conditions. And not content with achieving that, she saw to it that the prisoners received exercise, education and religious instruction, and useful work.

Certain that she was to continue to serve the imprisoned, Elizabeth Fry was equally adamant about how that service worked. "Much depends on the spirit in which the visitor enters upon her work," she wrote of her experiences within Newgate Prison. "It must be done in the spirit, not of judgment, but of mercy. She must not say in her heart, 'I am more holy than thou,' but must rather keep in perpetual remembrance that 'all have sinned and come short of the glory of God.' "[6]

## MERCY IN ACTION

Elizabeth Fry exemplified mercy in action, as did a relatively unknown contemporary of the apostle Paul named Onesiphorus. When Paul was imprisoned in Rome, the Christians in Asia Minor abandoned him, probably out of fear of being jailed themselves. The one exception was Onesiphorus, who, as Paul related in a letter to Timothy, "often refreshed me; he was not ashamed of my chains" (2 Tim. 1:16).

Through Paul's eyes, we see the compassion that Onesiphorus showered upon the apostle in the Roman jail and learn of the mercy he showed to those in the Christian church at Ephesus. Without any difficulty, we understand Paul's petition to the Lord that he grant Onesiphorus his mercy on the final day.

In the lives of the saints from the first century of Christianity to the present, mercy in action has been a wholehearted endeavor. And for it to be wholehearted, all merciful deeds must be done with good cheer (Rom. 12:8). There can be no dull, grudging sense of dutifulness about our behavior. We are serving others through a gift of the Spirit, and that knowledge alone should fill us with a contagious joy.

At first glance, this cheerfulness seems impossible to achieve. In being merciful and doing compassionate deeds, aren't we helping those in dire need and sin and distress? We have already joined the poor in spirit, and now we are being asked to minister to the sick and sinful and guilty, the shameful and honorless and disgraced. How can we possibly call this a "cheerful" burden?

The answer stands before us, eloquent in its simplicity and love. When we are merciful to others, we know the mercy of God. And it is his mercy that sanctifies our compassion and fills us with the desire to serve others cheerfully. Our compassion is nothing but a dim reflection of his own compassion, and our joy an imperfect mirror of his joy.

When a man seeks to join the Cisterian Order of the Strict Observance (Trappist), he stands before the community and is asked this ritual question: *Quid petis? What do you ask?*

*The mercy of God and of the Order* is his equally formal response. Of all that he could request, from the ecstasy of contemplation to the desire for Christian perfection, mercy is his answer. Nothing else will do, for through this gift, he can shoulder the burden of his sins and those of his fellow Trappists. He can seek divine forgiveness, be forgiven, and forgive those who have wronged him. He can reach out to his suffering brethren in compassion and express it in concrete deeds of mercy. He can bear with their faults, learn the ministry of silence and of confrontation. And he will grow to know the discipline, the transformation, the cheerfulness, and the love that makes this gift of the Spirit both notable and needed.

*The mercy of God and of the Order.* That is an excellent answer for us, too, as we seek to live as gentle members of the Body of Christ.

# 11. Healing: Ministering to Body, Mind, and Spirit

Bless the Lord, O my soul, and forget not all his benefits: who forgives all your iniquities; who heals all your diseases; who redeems your life from destruction; who crowns you with loving-kindness and tender mercies.

—PSALM 103:2–4

The third gift of the Spirit, which is crucial to developing gentleness, has a rich history, a complex structure, and diverse expression. Healing, on its most elemental level, is a return to the wholeness that Christ promised. Through sin, we separate ourselves from God, one another, and self. Having violated the laws of God, we are fractured, divided, wounded, sick, and hurting in our mind and body and spirit. And in our alienation from God, we become alienated from all else, within as well as without.

It is at this stage that we realize how important a part of God's salvation healing really is. If we take the Latin root word *salvare* literally, we find that it means "to save health." Healing is that saving of health that comes with being in accord with God and his purpose for us.

As Charles Allen stated in his inspirational book *God's Psychiatry*, healing means "bringing the person into a right relationship with the physical, mental, and spiritual laws of God."[1] Since it is God who creates life, it is his laws that govern every aspect of life. We must know the rules that govern our spirit as well as the physical and psychological ones governing our body and mind. Emotional understanding must be accompanied by spiritual truth and physical knowledge, for our body, mind, and spirit continually interact in a unity that we call the individual.

Whereas the body is the domain of medicine and the mind that of psychology, the spirit belongs to more than the discipline of theology, since it expresses itself through both the body and the mind. Concerned with the personal relationship with God, our spirit shapes the body and mind in accordance with that divine relationship.

Our deepest reality is as a spiritual being with a body and a mind. We love God and desire to obey him. We devote ourselves to his service and seek to know him better. We truly believe that God has a purpose for each of us, and we wish only to live in accordance with this purpose. To strive to learn and live God's purpose is to learn and live a life of salvation. To depart from it is harmful to our spiritual health, which ultimately affects our physical and mental well-being too.

In a Christian approach to healing, the basis of our spiritual health rests on our experiential relationship with God, our personal knowing of him, our communion with him that we then extend to others. Our spiritual development has a strong bearing on our psychological and physical development. Conversely, our spiritual difficulties will cause corresponding problems in the other two domains. And healing, to be successful, must begin in the spiritual realm. To use David's words, we heal by seeking to "restore the soul."

## THE SPIRITUAL WORLD

Before we can discuss the stages we move through in restoring the soul to health, we should take a step back and explore the world of the soul. In this pragmatic day and age, we shy away from considering that spiritual realm in which we can know both the love of God and the force of evil. A world apart, a distinct and separate reality, the spiritual realm, with its demons and angels, has been addressed by nearly every religion, and in Christianity from the writers of the Old Testament to contemporary evangelists.

Yet, many of us still find the concept of a spiritual world an expression of medieval poetic license. We have great difficulty believing in a realm as real as the physical one that is populated by demonic as well as angelic powers. We ignore Jesus' constant reminders of the workings of the Evil One, conveniently skipping over his temptations by the devil in the wilderness and his casting out of evil spirits and demons. We simply aren't comfortable with forthright statements about the existence of the spiritual world. Nor do we like to think that it has much to do with our "real" life here in the physical world. Occasionally, a contemporary voice addresses our response to this other world. Richard Lovelace is one such person; he continues to remind us,

Periods of renewal are times of vigorous activity both among agents of God and agents of darkness. Behind the scenes of earthly history in awakening areas, we can dimly discern the massing and movement of invisible troops of darkness and of light. While this may seem fanciful to anyone in the twentieth century, it is simply realistic according to the biblical world picture, in which the angels of God are portrayed as locked in combat with the occupying powers of darkness at critical junctures in the unfolding of world history.[2]

We tend to dismiss this description of the spiritual world as irrational and unscientific. Over the centuries, we've lost our certainty about its nature and our access to it as well. But our loss isn't limited to rejecting a spiritual reality filled with opposing forces of darkness and light. We have also lost a deeper understanding of Christian healing that is based in the spiritual realm as surely as in the scientific.

The noted historian Michael Grant, looking at the role of Jesus and his apostles as healers, found that this aspect of their ministry "was a hallowed activity possessing ancient and reverent associations."[3] And this hallowed activity took place in a world far removed from science and technology. There,

healing is secured by touching the healer or his garments; where resident healing power flows as a substance from one to another, and where healing potency is a commodity transferable to assistants; where saliva is applied to tongue and eyes, where the touch or grasp of the healer's hand, the supreme instrument of power, effects immediate cure; and . . . where reports of mighty works can bring fear that the Baptist is come back from the dead.[4]

In Jesus' time, the eternal and temporal worlds, the physical and the spiritual, had fused into one. Today, our perception may be different, but we, at the very least, still acknowledge the spiritual realm as one in which we can love God or rebel against him, sin and be forgiven, know sickness and be healed. It remains a world in which Satan constantly tries to frustrate God's purpose in our lives. David Watson reminds us bluntly that "there are a number of well-tried tactics of the Evil One that we need to understand. First, Satan seeks to destroy God's work by the direct attack of persecution, or by various assaults on the bodies, minds, and spirits of God's people."[5]

Our worldview may not include a fusing of the eternal and the temporal, but bridges span the gulf that we have created between the spiritual and the physical. "The experiences of the inner world are the prime realities that give us our approach to life, the basis for our widely varying emotions and feelings and values," Morton Kelsey wrote in describing how the temporal and eternal interact in our lives even today. "Sickness can force a reconsidering of the whole of one's life, and sacramental healing of one thing or another can be the opening to another realm of reality."[6]

Rufus Jones crossed one of these bridges during December 1922 after he was in a serious car accident and suffered severe injuries. While he was convalescing at home, he marveled at the healing process taking place in his body and felt "a 'restoration' of another sort had gone on. I seemed in a new way to be liberated from fears and anxieties and worries. I had entered into an unexpected tranquility and peace. More than that I had gained an immense increase of vitality and *vis viva*. Life had become a more joyous and radiant affair than I had ever known."[7]

Rufus Jones could never say exactly how he had moved from one realm to the other in healing, and finally attributed it to "a case of quiet mystical receptivity. Spiritual energies of a more or less permanent order flowed in and operated, as though God at my fountains far off had been raining."[8]

For this Quaker mystic, the soul stood on divine ground as concretely as the physical body did on more earthly soil. The inner and the outer world, the spiritual and the physical, the eternal and the temporal, were separate yet related levels of reality. His thinking was not far different from the great church fathers, who saw "humanity with one side joined to the physical world of matter, and the other immersed in the nonmaterial but even more real world-of-spirit, and the human soul or psyche as the instrument of communication between the two."[9]

In healing, we follow the soul back and forth in its communication between these two worlds. We seek to discover God's will for us and then relate it to our work, family, and friends. In health, we find harmony existing between our life and God's purpose. The life we live in our spirit corresponds with the life we live in our body and our mind; and most importantly, what we do as individuals corresponds with what God expects of us.

## BEING HEALED

In sickness, harmony no longer exists. Our illness may be physical, spiritual, emotional, or any combination thereof. Our lack of good health may originate from dietary, environmental, moral, viral, chemical, bacterial, genetic, or other physical, mental, or spiritual factors. But in Christian healing, the interrelatedness of body, mind, and spirit is of utmost importance, and wholeness remains the goal.

"God's plan for wholeness is clear," David Watson explains. "Through Christ we can be reconciled to God, and begin to know the healing of our relationship with him."[10] Once this relationship is healed, other types of healing on other levels can take place.

Healing of our relationship with God starts when we surrender to his sovereignty and acknowledge his power over all realms. By faith, we bow to a Power greater than we are, a Power that can do so many things, including healing the sicknesses that exist within us. And in bowing to this Power, we also surrender to his Son, who is called Savior, which means Healer. We know that the physician can cure our body, and the psychiatrist our mind. But we seek the wholeness that only Christ can give. So our first step in the healing of our relationship with God and being healed begins in surrender.

We recognize the basis of our illness and turn to God for his help. We take responsibility for our sickness, when appropriate. And we don't assume false responsibility out of misplaced humility or guilt. When speaking of illness, we often display an unfortunate tendency to lay the blame for being ill on the sick individual. Although we frequently do help to create our physical, emotional, and spiritual sicknesses, we are not always responsible.

Less frequently but just as erroneously, we may place full responsibility for illness on God. To this charge, Dennis and Matthew Linn in their warm and insightful book *Healing Life's Hurts* respond with refreshing directness: "Sickness like injustice is evil. God doesn't send sickness any more than he sends injustice. When Jesus tells me to do the same things that he does (John 14:12), Jesus is telling me to be a healer like him and to wage war on sickness."[11]

One of the most effective ways to wage war on sickness is through prayer. Yet, even in prayer, we run into difficulties. In praying for the recovery of our health and to be cured of what ails us, we face the possibility of cutting off true communication with God rather than deepening it. Although there is nothing wrong in praying for health, in such a prayer we must be careful not to place our own will before God's.

We need to ask him to show us the path he wants us to follow. And when approaching him in prayer, we must realize that healing may not be the divine answer at that moment in our life. We may not like hearing it, but Christ does call some of us to redemptive suffering in which we grow spiritually from the illness we experience.

The lessons taught by illness are many and vary from case to case. We may relearn our need for dependence upon God or may renew our flagging commitment to be poor in spirit. Yet there are times when we cannot fathom God's will. We watch an innocent child suffer and ask why this is so. I don't pretend to have any answer other than knowing God truly does move in ways beyond my understanding. I choose to accept on faith, on logic, and on feeling that dreadful illnesses do happen to the just and unjust because an all-powerful yet personal God deems it so. My prayers for the ill have become over time less a request for healing and more a seeking to discover and obey God's will, to accept his decision and abide with him.

Prayer as a crucial part of healing can only draw us closer to God. We begin to feel his love and trust him with our fears and wants and desires. And along with an honest expression of these feelings, we accept what he wants for our life, be it suffering or freedom from it.

Although prayer leads us toward reconciliation, it alone cannot heal our relationship with God. Confession, that admission of sin and heartfelt cry for forgiveness, must follow. Since sin separates us from God and one another, confessing our sins to God and each other heals the wounds that our sin has caused. We act in a deliberate manner to confess both to God and to one another, as Scripture has outlined. We seek forgiveness and pray that we will recognize and know it.

"The Discipline of confession brings an end to pretense," Richard Foster writes in *Celebration of Discipline*. "God is calling into being a church that can openly confess its frail humanity and know the forgiving and empowering graces of Christ. Honesty leads to confession, and confession leads to change."[12]

And that change centers on our awareness that we no longer are alone. We now belong to the Body of Christ. And through our acceptance of a saving Christ, we can be reconciled with the Father. Our relationship with God will now be healed, and we will know a new liberating force that comes with the release of God's healing power.

In those rare moments of grace when we feel this healing that approaches wholeness, we recognize that we, too, are granted the Spirit-given ability to restore the soul, ours as well as others. Through our reconciled beings, Christ uses us, his human instruments, to heal others physically, emotionally, or spiritually.

## LIVING IN THE SHADOW OF CHRIST

By releasing others from physical, emotional, or demonic illness, we live in the healing shadow of Christ. In the early church, he used many of us as surrogate healers, but today such healing appears to be rare and restricted to a very few.

When the apostle Paul spoke of the gifts of healings (1 Cor. 12:9), interestingly enough he used the double plural, indicating several levels and types of cures granted through the Spirit. We have already seen the intricate relationships that exist between the physical, mental, and spiritual as well as between God, self, and others. The gifts of healings cover all of these, from our healed relationship with God to that within self and with others.

In this context, the dramatic, God-given ability to heal others becomes one way in which we can live in the shadow of Christ. There are other ways we can be used as healers, beginning with our day-to-day responsibility to minister to our own body, mind, and spirit. In the Bible, we are given an excellent guide to healthful living, complete with physical, mental, and moral counsel. From diet and sleep to work and recreation, from family life and marriage to imagination and thoughts, Scripture reveals God's laws to us.

Also, in these pages, we are given psychological injunctions, physical regulations, precepts for social behavior, and guidelines for spiritual growth. We need only accept and follow them to be healed of what Paul Tillich rightly describes as "the torturing anxiety in the depths of our hearts, the restlessness which never ceases moving and whipping us, the unordered desires and the hidden repressions which return as poisonous hate, the hostility against ourselves and others, against life itself, the hidden will to death."[13]

We can live in Christ's shadow and know yet another aspect of healing when we minister to our neighbor's body, mind, and spirit as demanded in the Word. In *Desert Wisdom,* a collection of sayings from the desert fathers, we learn in this simple little story what the healing ministry to others encompasses. Listen.

A brother who was insulted by another brother came to Abba Sisoes, and said to him: I was hurt by my brother, and I want to avenge myself. The old man tried to console him and said: Don't do that, my child. Rather leave vengeance to God. But he said: I will not quit until I avenge myself. Then the old man said: Let us pray, brother; and standing up, he said: O God, we no longer need you to take care of us since we now avenge ourselves. Hearing these words, the brother fell at the feet of the old man and said: I am not going to fight with my brother any more. Forgive me, Abba.[14]

The healing ministry consists of placing our neighbor before ourselves. It means listening to others' needs and addressing them in a loving manner, accepting the pain or hurt or humiliation that they have given us and returning forgiveness in its stead. It's a willingness to assist others, even by doing something as small as taking a reluctant person to a doctor or recommending a specialist. Or it may consist of devoting ourselves in voluntary service to those in an understaffed nursing home or to the chronically ill on a hospital ward. We could also open ourselves to sharing advice that is God-centered and God-given or graciously accept the burden of receiving another's confession.

Each day we encounter challenging ways in which we can help others with our practical acts of healing. We choose, in this ministry, to live in Christ's shadow and become more like him. When we are healed, we love Jesus more and he loves more through us. In his shadow, those people whom we touch he also touches, restoring our soul and theirs, the human relationship and the divine.

One of my favorite verses, sung by the monks of Weston Priory, deals with the fruit of living in Christ's shadow. Singing the Gospel of Matthew, the brothers tell us of Jesus' healing servanthood: "Come to me . . . for I am gentle . . . and you will find rest for your souls" (Matt. 11:28–29). No insistence. No threats. Only a listening heart ready to instruct and succor, serve and forgive.

It is in this scriptural passage that I understand best the connection between the healing ministry and gentleness. *Gentle* is translated "restful" in the Syriac New Testament,[15] which is not surprising, for through healing we do find a quiet and soothing restfulness in the presence of God, ourselves, and others.

This aspect of gentleness is the outgrowth of divine and human ministering to body, mind, and spirit. The grace that comes upon us from serving and being served, it anticipates the wholeness we will know in God someday. Springing from the power of reconciliation, forgiveness, and love, restfulness marks us as finally being among the gentle.

# 12. Giving: Developing A Practical Covenant

Whatever a man would gladly have that he relinquishes and goes without for God's love, be it something material or spiritual, he will find all of it in God.

—MEISTER ECKHART

Seven centuries ago, a young, well-to-do merchant turned his back on his comfortable life in the city of Assisi and went to a cave in the hills above town to become a man of prayer. When he emerged, the plight of the poor filled many of his waking thoughts. He began giving the less fortunate food from his mother's table, coins from his purse, and on more than one occasion, even the shirt off his back. Once, he traveled to Rome to join the beggars, so that he would know what misery and destitution they experienced every day.

In others' eyes, his spirit appeared to be filled with saintly generosity. But Francis of Assisi knew this impression of himself to be false. Giving to the poor came easily to him, but it brought him no closer to practicing true generosity of the spirit. This man of prayer had begun to uncover his weaknesses, and numbering greatest among them was the revulsion he felt toward lepers.

In thirteenth-century Catholic Italy, lepers had become objects of pious care, and Francis saw them often near the hospital in Assisi. The stench of their diseased bodies filled him with horror. Never could he bring himself to give them alms unless he had someone else hand it to them.

Yet, Francis knew that to continue to grow spiritually he must give to those whom he feared and disliked most. The struggle that ensued within him culminated one afternoon when he met a leper on the road outside Assisi. Fighting the nausea that threatened to overcome him, Francis placed a coin in the leper's rotting hand,

and with a supreme effort of will, kissed the ravaged fingers Continuing on his way, Francis knew a joy he hadn't experienced before. The next morning found him at the gate of the hospital, where he gave alms and embraced and visited with the lepers within.[1]

In a life devoted to utilizing the gift of giving, this beloved saint set an example few of us haved dared to imitate. Often we are too easily content with practicing one aspect or another of this spiritual gift without challenging ourselves, as Francis did, to overcome our greatest failing in giving of ourselves and our resources. We settle for tithing, sending occasional checks to various relief agencies, donating used clothing, and doing community service work. But we stop there, looking no further into what this gift of giving really encompasses.

Certainly, giving includes all volunteer work and material generosity that help our brothers and sisters. Yet, this Spirit-given and Spirit-driven ability to give is more than a ministry of money and time. As a gift of God, giving involves a generosity of spirit as well as of pocketbook, a sharing of ourselves as well as our possessions, an exercise of our spiritual strengths as well as our fiscal ones.

## SINGLENESS OF MIND

Giving is one of the most practical covenants made between God and his creations. In giving, God works through us to serve others, which, in turn, furthers God's work. Although giving is an action that we take, it is only a talent and not a God-given gift until we understand that everything, including our giving, is God's to give and is done for his glory. When we exercise the gift of giving, we do so for one purpose: to glorify him.

"For God does not give, he has never given any gift so that we might have it and then rest upon it; but all the gifts he ever gave in heaven and on earth he gave so that he might give us the one gift that is himself," Meister Eckhart declared in one of his conversations when he was Vicar of Thuringia. He went on to explain, "All the works God has ever performed in heaven and on earth he performed for the sake of one work, so that he might perform that, and it is to be himself blessed, so that he may make us blessed."[2]

In giving, which is also the most pragmatic gift related to gentleness, we must learn not to focus on the action itself but single-mindedly on God instead. We give with our eyes fixed solely on God, seeking no other vision but him. Christ taught us how: "Take heed that you do not give your alms before men, to be seen of them; . . . when you do give alms, sound no trumpet before you, as the hypocrites do in the synagogues and in the streets, that they may be praised by men. . . . But when you give alms, do not let your left hand know what your right hand is doing, so that your alms may be in secret" (Matt. 6:1–4).

We are to give with no self-seeking motives. We contribute to God's people so that we may do him honor. We are obeying his Son's repeated command to feed his sheep on the most basic level with food and clothing and shelter, and on the deepest level with spiritual sustenance. For when we act in the image of the Giver, we are free to sustain others bodily, emotionally, and spiritually as the need arises. The benefits that he bestows upon us we now desire to share with our fellow humans. Our conduct is beginning to resemble his conduct, and our giving reflects but a small portion of his.

With this spiritual gift, God's concern rests more upon *why* we give than *what* we give. Although Christ promised us more than once that our reward for giving will be great, we must give out of love for him and not out of a selfish desire for a hundred fold return on our generosity. "My eyes are ever toward the Lord," the psalmist cried (Ps. 25:15). In giving, our eyes cannot turn away from him toward heavenly rewards or earthly acclaim. They must remain fixed upon him alone.

Through prayer, we stay in single-minded contact with the divine center of our lives. And in this spirit of prayer, the generosity that imitates Christ's generosity takes hold and thrives. All aspects of our lives become a gift to share rather than to possess. We reach out to the Giver of all life and receive a desire to give to our neighbor in return. Our singleness of mind has opened our hearts.

## OPENNESS OF HEART

Giving is a spiritual gift centering on relationships. In opening our hearts, we are making room for friends and strangers alike to share our homes, our possessions, our emotions, our dreams, and our love. We are creating a nurturing space where we can strive to meet their needs by utilizing the gift of giving. It is also a space where both strangers and enemies may become our friends, for openness of heart is an unwritten invitation to others to enter into our lives.

This invitation has been called by different names over time, none better than hospitality. "It is one of the richest biblical terms that can deepen and broaden our insight in our relationships to our fellow human beings," Henri Nouwen wrote about hospitality in *Reaching Out.* [3]

From Genesis to the Epistles, providing a warm and welcome haven for guests was frequently enacted and commanded. Through these biblical stories, we learn not just that "hospitality is an important virtue, but even more, that in the context of hospitality, guest and host can reveal their most precious gifts and bring new life to each other."[4]

Hospitality growing out of scriptural tradition breaks down the boundaries between friend and stranger as well as between enemies. It is a sharing of our physical, mental, and spiritual world with those we have grown afraid to know better. By opening our hearts and offering others a meal, a ride, overnight lodging, a receptive attitude, and honest conversation, we dismantle the walls of fear and hostility we have erected to protect ourselves, our beliefs, and our possessions.

We are not seeking to impress others with who we are or what we have, but to appreciate them as they are. It doesn't matter whether our resources are meager or substantial. True hospitality can only be offered with the heart. In his deeply moving book *The City of Joy,* Dominique Lapierre shares so memorable an account of the hospitality received by the Hasari Pal family in Calcutta that it is best quoted in full:

The Pals had no idea where to go next. They crossed the great bridge and simply kept on walking. It was dark but despite the late hour, the streets were still full of people. Bewildered by the throngs that milled about like ants, jostling each other and shouting, they reached a place in the very heart of the city. Pitiful in her poor peasant sari, Aloka had taken her youngest son in her arms and held her daughter by her hand. Manooj, the eldest boy, walked in front with his father. They were so afraid of losing each other that they called out constantly to one another in the darkness. The pavement was littered with sleeping people, wrapped from head to toe in bits of *khadi* cloth. They looked like corpses. As soon as they found an empty space, the Pals stopped to rest a while. A family was camping nearby. The mother was roasting *chapatis* on a portable stove. She and her family came from Madras. Fortunately, they spoke a few words of Hindi, a language Hasari could vaguely understand. They too had left the countryside for the mirage of Calcutta. They offered the Pals a hot griddle cake and swept a corner of the pavement so that the newcomers could settle themselves next to them. The strangers' hospitality brought new warmth to the peasant's heart. At least his family would be safe in their company until he found work.[5]

As difficult as it is to show hospitality to strangers, opening our hearts to the despised requires even more effort and prayer. We've seen how Saint Francis grew by reaching out to the lepers of Assisi. But hospitality since Old Testament times has been urged for other, more supernatural reasons. "Do not neglect to show hospitality to strangers," we are warned by the anonymous writer of the Letter to the Hebrews. "For thereby some have entertained angels unawares" (Heb. 13:2).

This had happened to Abraham when he treated the three strangers at Mamre hospitably (Gen. 18:1–15), to the widow at Zarephath (1 Kings 17:9–24), and to the two travelers on the road to Emmaus after the Crucifixion (Luke 24:13–35).

In the days of Gregory the Great, we find the first of many stories dealing with God's testing of our hospitality. The monk Martyrius met a leper by the wayside, who from pain and sickness had fallen to the ground and could drag himself no farther. The monk wrapped the man in his cloak and carried him to his monastery. But as he walked along, the leper changed in his arms to Jesus and rose to heaven, blessing the hospitable monk.[6] In Abba Agathon's case, the leper was an angel of God who first put him through a number of exasperating tests before revealing his true identity.[7] And Saint Julian, Saint Leo IX, and the Blessed Colombini all had similar encounters.

In each case, hospitality became the means to see beyond superficial appearances. In yielding to a hospitable attitude toward the despised, we are, in fact, embracing that of God in others. In opening our hearts to the least of his creatures, we are showing our love for the Creator himself.

Opening our hearts to the despised offers us a priceless opportunity for growth, and so does opening our hearts to our enemies. When Jesus commanded us to love our neighbor, he made it clear that we are also to love our enemy: "Bless them that curse you, do good to them that hate you, and pray for them which despitefully use you, and persecute you" (Matt. 5:44).

Our natural reaction is to close our hearts to those who can pierce them, to barricade our possessions behind protective walls, to make every aspect of our lives invulnerable to attack. The thought of sharing and distributing our blessings with our enemies appears outrageous until we look at the example the Lord set as gracious host in the Psalm of David: "Thou preparest a table before me in the presence of my enemies" (Ps. 23:5).

Our invulnerability can only come by way of hospitality. When we open our hearts to God and to *all* others, we know God's goodness, including his protective love. We have nothing to fear now, for we can give on the level he wishes us to, with our hearts as well as our purses, to our enemies as well as to those we love.

## LIVING SIMPLY

When we are concerned with amassing wealth beyond our needs, when we extravagantly consume resources and are consumed, in turn, by the passion to possess, our lives have moved from the simplicity that is God-ordained toward a selfishness that is, in itself, an outright rejection of God. We no longer live with what Thomas Kelly called that "singleness of eye, from a holy

Center where the breath and stillness of Eternity are heavy upon us and we are wholly yielded to Him."[8]

Without this focus, which alone simplifies our life, we cannot exercise the gift of giving to any significant degree. We become so concerned with our outward affairs, we find that we aren't attentive to God's presence and guidance and will. In the crowded hours of our lives, we lose sight of God's gifts to us and become deaf to his voice. We accumulate rather than let go, clutching our possessions more tightly while closing our hearts to the need of others.

To return to genuine caring and sharing of ourselves and our resources, we have little choice but to embrace living simply. And to do this properly means that we first must overcome certain destructive attitudes that, unfortunately, are all too prevalent in our society today. These attitudes are closely related. Covetousness, greed, and hoarding are distortions of the positive attitudes of ambition, industry, and prudence.

In covetousness, the legitimate and worthy drive to provide ourselves and our families with the necessities to live escalates into an inordinate desire to possess material goods. Enslaved to acquiring the things of this world, covetous persons effectively seal themselves off from Christ and others.

The greedy move one step beyond the desires of the covetous. They are never satisfied with the amount of goods they have amassed and are always seeking more. The "New! Improved! More Advanced!" style of advertising has been designed to arouse the greedy among us. Need has little to do with their purchases. Possessions reflect the center of their lives, and they choose to serve them rather than God.

Hoarding is the taking of greed and covetousness to the extreme. The individual hoards worldly goods in direct disobedience to Christ's command: "Lay not up for yourselves treasures upon earth, where moth and rust corrupt and thieves break through and steal." Rather, we are to search elsewhere. "But lay up for yourselves treasures in heaven, where neither moth nor rust corrupt, and where thieves do not break through nor steal," he tells us instead. "For where your treasure is, there will your heart be also" (Matt. 6:19–21).

When our hearts are centered on God, we realize that there is nothing inherently wrong with earthly goods. They have been given to us to benefit others. It is when we use our possessions as barriers between ourselves and God that our lives become hopelessly complex. In that complexity, the God-given ability to give to others is eclipsed by our obsessions with accumulating what we don't need but have grown to desire and love.

Living simply means to exist in the absence of all that is unnecessary. It is living in this world with an appreciation of the fine, functional, and good things of life. Yet, this appreciation must include a freedom from care and anxiety. As Thomas Merton reminds us, living simply means that we use created things "without selfishness, without fear, without afterthought, and with perfect gratitude and confidence and love of God".[9]

Loving God, we trust him with our future and know that our security resides in him, not in our worldly possessions. We are not fearful of the knowledge that the Kingdom of God must always come before our earthly concerns. We renounce wastefulness and oppose extravagance in our lives, choosing necessities rather than luxuries, service to God rather than slavery to the selfish dictates of the world, and genuine celebration over superfluity. With our lives thus simplified, we are now capable of managing on less and giving away more.

## BEING A GOOD STEWARD

If I walk due north of my house, I cross the boundary between the national forest and Mescalero Apache Reservation. Climbing upward and reaching the eleven-thousand-foot mark on the mountain, I can look southwest over an extensive, barren intermountain region. On a cloudless day, the long, irregular shape of white gypsum dunes glitters in strange contrast to the brown drabness of the high desert surrounding it. From this distance and height, the immense size of the White Sands Proving Grounds is dwarfed, and its purpose obscured. I know that somewhere in its expanse a marker stands, commemorating the site of the first atomic explosion.

Hiroshima. Nagasaki. The blinding millisecond glare with its familiar mushroom shape burned upon the retina of the mind's eye. The insanity and incessant threat of the nuclear arms race. The fear and finally the prayer: "If it be so, our God whom we serve is able to deliver us from the burning fiery furnace; and he will deliver us out of your hand, O king" (Dan. 3:17).

Slowly, my inner vision turns from the holocaust to the holistic. I look downward to the ancient mountain on which I stand, and I sense that here, in this remote corner of an uncharted and unknown universe, earth and sky, body and mind, matter and spirit, inner experience and the outer world meet and are one. I feel the interconnectedness of all life systems and my role as creative participant within this integrated world.

When the Lord gave us "dominion over the fish of the sea, and over the fowl of the air, and over every living thing that moves upon the earth" (Gen. 1:28), he meant us to be neither manipulators nor proprietors. We are the stewards of this earth and its resources, responsible to God as our Creator, to the earth which he has created, and to our fellow humans with whom we must share what God has entrusted to our care.

To be faithful stewards, we must strive to conserve the earth's finite resources, to develop them according to God's purpose, and to distribute them fairly in the service of others. By destroying the environment, being wasteful, and failing to share our resources justly with others, we are abusing our stewardship as well as our relationship with God, the natural world, and others.

Our stewardship is meant to be both benevolent and peaceful. Through God's gifts, we foreshadow that world of which the prophet Isaiah spoke, where

> The wolf shall dwell with the lamb,
> and the leopard shall lie down with the kid,
> And the calf and the lion and the fatling together,
> and a little child shall lead them.

The cow and the bear shall feed;
their young shall lie down together;
and the lion shall eat straw like the ox.
The suckling child shall play over the hole
of the asp, and the weaned child shall put
his hand on the adder's den.
They shall not hurt or destroy in all my holy
mountain; for the earth shall be full of the
knowledge of the Lord, as the waters cover the
sea.

(Isa. 11:6–9)

With this vision of good stewardship, we are compelled to care for and share with our neighbors. We can give of ourselves and our goods because we feel no attachment to them, only our responsibility to God. This caring is the overriding feeling we experience once we have accepted the spiritual gift of giving wholeheartedly. And sharing is its legitimate expression, touching our every moment with the need to give.

Being a good steward is a way to channel giving toward God's purpose. It involves examining our life more closely than is sometimes comfortable for us. It also involves a realistic appraisal of all that we can do to act as responsible caretakers of this earth and one another. Do we conserve energy in our house or with the car we drive? Are our investments consistent with promoting ecological wholeness? Do we donate our money, talents, and time to activities that seek to renew the land and its resources? What actions are we taking to alleviate the misery of the poor, the voiceless, the exploited, and the powerless in our society? What are we, who have been granted so much by God, giving to the less fortunate in his name? Good stewardship calls for us to be responsible participants in this world; with the gift of giving, we can fulfill that responsibility correctly.[10]

## THESE GENTLE GIFTS

The gifts of giving, healing, mercy, and humility are Spirit-given, and ultimately, Spirit-directed. Exercised properly, they help us lead our lives according to his will. And it is his will that we should commit ourselves to one another in loving service.

Although I have treated these four gifts individually, they are interconnected in a most powerful way. Like four tapers of a candelabra, humility, mercy, healing, and giving are separate yet interrelated. Each sheds light on its own, but together they illuminate something more than a single spiritual gift.

"Every gift is vital within the body of Christ," David Watson states. "Each needs the other."[11] Alone, these four gifts of the Spirit fulfill a specific purpose of God's. Together, they transcend that individual purpose by preparing us to be living expressions of that fruit of the Spirit we call gentleness.

# IV.  BEARING FRUIT

By this my Father is glorified, that you bear much fruit,
and so prove to be my disciple.

—JOHN 15:8

# 13. Power: Carrying Out the Charge

Dear Lord, let your Spirit give me the power to overcome all hesitation, to take away all fear, and to remove all shyness. May your Spirit help me respond gratefully to you, speak freely about you to everyone I meet, and act courageously to let your Kingdom come.

—HENRI NOUWEN

The meetinghouse was silent except for the slow, steady breathing of the fellowship joined together for worship. We were gathered to wait upon the Lord, to share that intimate sense of his presence, to feel him among us, strengthening, uplifting, enlightening, renewing us in the living Spirit.

I shall never forget that first meeting when I actually felt the Spirit descend upon us, uniting us to one another and to God. The silence was deafening, the holy power shattering. Time was eclipsed and, losing its linear dimensions, looped in upon itself. The eighteenth-century Quakers who had worshiped in this meetinghouse, the solitary desert fathers, the medieval Christian mystics, the shaken gathering of first-century disciples who were filled with the Holy Spirit, the apostles in the Jerusalem streets at Pentecost, the hymn writers and prophets of ancient Israel merged and blended into a blessed household beyond time, becoming "a dwelling place of God in the Spirit" (Eph. 2:22).

God has filled and will continue filling his creatures with the Spirit, renewing, strengthening, and deepening our communion, our love, and its expression. The touch of the Spirit within us is also empowering. Thomas Kelly put it beautifully when he wrote that

maturing experience brings awareness of being met and tutored, purged and disciplined, simplified and made pliant in His holy will by a power waiting within us. For God Himself works in our souls, in their deepest depths, taking increasing control as we are progressively willing to be prepared for His wonder. We cease trying to make ourselves the dictators and God the listeners, and become the joyful listeners to Him, the Master Who does all things well.[1]

We now live in the power of the Spirit, a power that comes from the crucified, risen, and glorified Christ. Between the first Easter and the Ascension, Jesus showed us this power before bestowing it upon his apostles. Since then, it has become the inheritance of every person who dares to live Christianity to its fullest, and as Christians we are incomplete without it.

The power of the Spirit fulfills Jesus' promise that he will bring forth fruit through us. With this power, we can think and believe, speak and act with gentleness and manifest it in our lives daily.

## NOT OF THIS WORLD

The power that produces the fruit of gentleness is heavenly rather than earthly. It has little to do with the dominion and control vested in the authorities and leaders of civil governments in this world. It takes no satisfaction in manipulating, developing, or organizing the people, events, and destiny of a corporation, state, nation, or continent. Neither is earthly power the mirror image of a more celestial force. Rather, it is the antithesis of it.

Receiving the power of the Spirit is a lesson in powerlessness. "For we cannot lift up a hand, or stir a foot, but by a power that is lent us from God," William Law wrote with humbling accuracy in his *A Serious Call to a Devout and Holy Life.* [2] We do not possess this power, but through Christ, we are granted its use to act less as dictators and more as Kelly's joyful listeners.

Unlike the pure goodness of spiritual power, earthly power can be used as a force either for good or for evil. Expressed creatively, righteously, and cooperatively, worldly power can and does build cities and nations, feed the hungry, and shelter the homeless. It can also develop community and organize society, execute justice, and encourage more benevolent human enterprise and achievement. Misused, earthly power can release terror of demonic proportions, reaping destruction in our personal and professional lives, in homes and states and nations throughout the world. "Therefore, the social authorities should be accepted as guarantees of external order," Paul Tillich advises us, "but not as those which determine the meaning of our lives."[3]

As we continue to develop gentleness in our lives, we give increasing control to God and dedicate ourselves to doing his will. He alone determines the meaning of our lives now. We have learned to wait upon him, to continually open ourselves to his presence, to be renewed—not once as in our baptism—but over and over again in each and every moment of the day. Borrowing David Watson's words, we have found that the meaning of our lives rests in recapturing "the vision of daring living for the Lord, throwing ourselves totally upon the power of his Spirit, without whom we are nothing."[4]

We are powerless, and our response is to prepare ourselves to receive the power of the Spirit, knowing it will be granted to us if we but ask. Yet, as I discovered during one of the bleakest periods of my life, asking is usually farthest from our minds when we most need to turn to God for his help.

Several years ago, with the breakdown and collapse of my first marriage, I knew the feeling of powerlessness in almost every area of my life, and I despised it. My job, friendships, home life, financial security, and relationship with my children felt as though they were slipping beyond my control, and in anger and frustration, I not only lashed out and inflicted hurt on those around me, but I also turned my back firmly on God.

Fragile illusions of earthly power had disappeared, and I rejected the powerlessness that God demanded of me. I refused to throw myself upon his power; I felt I had too little of "my own" to begin with. More than once I gritted my teeth and vowed never to be powerless again.

But in turning my back upon God, I had forgotten that he is omnipresent. I continued to face him, but in my pain and anguish, I refused to see him. His creative power had already come into the heart of my life, but I refused to acknowledge that also. Yet, ever so slowly, in the mysterious way that is the power of the Living Presence within each of us, I began to see the Divine Light, to hear his voice and feel his power once again, tolerant, loving, long-suffering, working quietly to strengthen me where I was weakest, to turn my anger to love and my pain into communion with and commitment to him again.

I learned that to grow spiritually I had to embrace the power-lessness he required of me. And in becoming willingly powerless for him, I discovered that his power strengthens as no earthly power, good or evil, can. Every page of the Old Testament speaks directly of the mighty strength of God's power. In the New Testament, we also see the strengthening power of the conquering Christ. And in our lives, we find that the source of power is Christ, and the way to experience that power is to live, devoid of our own selfish desire for power, in him.

With our own strength of character, we can accomplish little in the way of spiritual growth. With total dependence upon Christ, we gain his strength and something more. We begin to know that the power of the Spirit ranges from the mightiness of strength to infinite gentleness.

His is the strength that disarms the principalities and powers, and the gentleness that tends the flock as only a good shepherd can. "We should never be afraid, therefore, that the gentleness of the Spirit means weakness of character," Jerry Bridges counsels us. "It takes strength, God's strength, to be truly gentle."[5]

## THE POWER OF GENTLENESS

To put the biblical command to be gentle into action in our lives we need the power of the Spirit. With it, we can live a life free of the fear of persecution, suffering, and punishment; we know the end of bitterness and resentment, too. The power that comes from the Spirit enables us to grow in courage, wisdom, and responsibility to and for others.

"We cannot create peace and joy, but the Spirit of Christ can fill us with a peace and joy which is not of this world," Henri Nouwen shared in *A Cry for Mercy*. "The Spirit of Christ burns away our many fears and anxieties and sets us free to move wherever we are sent. That is the great liberation of Pentecost."[6]

The Spirit's power is a liberating force that knows no limits. It raises each of us to our full spiritual height, as God, working through us, helps us conquer our fear of the dangers we face in building the Kingdom of God here on earth. When his power invades us, we are transformed into disciples who are willing to follow even in those places we would rather not venture.

We are used by the Spirit to do God's will through acts of service. In other words, we know God's power in our life through the gentleness of our service to others in his name. We go where he wishes us to go, and we help in the ways that he determines. And in this continuous movement of discipleship, we learn of the paradoxical nature of the power of gentleness. At the same time that we are torn loose of our personal but selfish fears, we gain a divine but painful concern for the world. "He plucks the world out of our hearts, loosening the chains of attachment," Thomas Kelly wrote. "And He hurls the world into our hearts, where we and He together carry it in infinitely tender love."[7]

Graced with this divine concern for others, we can now carry out the charge given to us to proclaim the advent of the Kingdom of God. More importantly, we can confirm it every moment we live by expressing the power of gentleness. And we best manifest this spiritual power when we recognize ourselves as responsible for the good of others, for their temporal fulfillment and, ultimately, for their eternal salvation.

With this world hurled into our hearts, we express the power of gentleness most effectively when we know we are one another's keepers and act accordingly. The starvation in the Sahel, the guerrilla warfare in Central America and Afghanistan, the racial injustice in South Africa, the killing fields of Cambodia, and the urban decay and feminization of poverty in American cities and towns should not be remote events barely causing a ripple across the smooth surface of our lives. Economic, political, and cultural ties bind the world more tightly together today, so that what happens across the globe or across the city is now our responsibility.

Utilizing the power of gentleness is an individual matter concerned with meeting the physical, psychological, and spiritual needs of others. This service to others becomes the driving wedge in our proclaiming the coming Kingdom of God. In this world but no longer attached to it, we see our actions as bearing witness to a heavenly Power, who is the ultimate expression of truth, justice, love, and, yes, gentleness.

We realize that to bear witness to him and to serve as he demands, we must increase rather than decrease our responsibility to and for our fellow humans. "The Christian cannot be fully what he is meant to be in the modern world if he is not in some way interested in *building a better society,* free of war, of racial and social injustice, of poverty, and of discrimination," declared Thomas Merton.[8]

We cannot evade our responsibility by withdrawing from the world. As Thomas Kelly put it in his inimitable way, neither can we falsely seek "a life of wallowing in ecstasies of spiritual sensuality while cries of the needy world go unheeded."[9] God grants us the power of the Holy Spirit. We really have no choice but to use it as fully as we possibly can. He asks so much of us, yet he gives so much through us in return.

## THE WAY OF POWER

In harnessing the power of gentleness, radical change will take place within us as well as in the way we treat others. Our vision of gentleness, illuminated by divine power, will help us act on what we have glimpsed, altering our lives as well as our hearts.

"My soul does not find itself unless it acts," Merton stated in an essay on the relationship between being and doing.[10] Our commitment to gentleness seeks its natural outlet in work. Acting gently, in turn, strengthens our growing commitment. The cycle of belief fueling action, which then renews and deepens our understanding yet again, becomes the way of power working in our lives.

Through the Spirit, our soul begins to see what is meant by gentleness. Clinging to this vision, we enact it in our lives and find, to our surprise, that we already see more clearly how better we may live gentleness. Action, vision, and deeper insight escalate and fuse, so that we recognize both the widening scope of gentleness needed in our lives and the conditions demanded to accomplish it.

Empowered by the Spirit, the quality of our actions bears direct witness to the gentleness of God. What we tell others about God's gentleness in our lives is less convincing than how we live that gentleness. Truly gentle Christians, who are filled with the power of the Spirit, will become worthy signposts, pointing to divine gentleness by the way they treat those in the world around them. Although teaching, preaching, and writing are valid ways of proclaiming God's gentleness, the most effective sermon is the manner in which we act to radiate the divine sparks.

In Scripture, we can find all the guidelines we need to treat others with gentleness. There is no better place to begin than Isaiah's prophecy of gentleness that Christ fulfilled: "He will not break a bruised reed or quench a smoldering wick, till he brings justice to victory" (Matt. 12:20). We are told here how gently Jesus deals with those who are weak or suffering. He doesn't use the force of his power, preferring instead to reconcile the broken and strengthen the faltering.

Illustrations of Jesus' gentleness toward the spiritually immature and uncertain abound in the Gospels. The sinners who anointed his feet with tears and perfumed oil, the Samaritan woman at the village well, the seventy who returned to him in joy over the success of their mission, the anxious sister Martha, and the adulteress all encountered his gentleness even as he rebuked them. He clearly saw their weaknesses and faults, but rather than berate them, he combined understanding with gentle counsel.

So too are we to act toward others. "Gentleness will demonstrate respect for the personal dignity of the other person. Where necessary, it will seek to change a wrong opinion or attitude by persuasion and kindness, not by domination or intimidation. It will studiously avoid coercion by threatening either directly or indirectly," explains Jerry Bridges in *The Practice of Godliness*. [11] This is the way of power in gentleness; its strength lies in the correct use of power and not its abuse.

In Paul's first letter to the immature congregation in Thessalonica, we find more words of wisdom about the proper exercise of gentleness. Comparing his missionary work among them to the gentleness of a nurse caring for a child, the apostle reminded them that gentleness includes a readiness "to share with you not only the gospel of God but also our own selves" (1 Thess. 2:8). There is an openness and vulnerability to the gentle person, who has placed himself or herself in God's power.

Although gentle Christians are vulnerable, they refuse to feel threatened by opposition or resentful toward those who disagree with them. In his second letter to his younger helper Timothy, Paul included in his practical advice for Christian leadership the necessity of "correcting his opponents with gentleness" (2 Tim. 2:25). With all power resting in God's hands, we must seek only to instruct others gently and let the Spirit work to remove the opposition or source of disagreement.

Gentleness is an active part of any Christian's duty. In his letter to Titus, Paul once again appealed to his fellow missionary "to be gentle, and to show perfect courtesy toward all men" (Titus 3:2). In the troublesome atmosphere of Crete, whose people were notorious for their aggressive quarreling, this advice to Titus is particularly telling. The gentle Christian is someone under God's control, bearing wrongs done to him or her graciously while remaining willing to help others who have been wronged.

Christians trying to live the ethical life outlined by Jesus in the Sermon on the Mount have yet another duty to others: "Brethren, if a man is overtaken in any trespass, you who are spiritual should restore him in a spirit of gentleness" (Gal. 6:1). Again, we are to imitate Christ, who restores our soul and reconciles us to him with a firm touch that is always gentle. Our words do not need to wound with their sharp edges, nor our manners with their cold disregard. Gentleness enlightens the wrongdoer and encourages the wayward to return with us to the Father.

Underlying this spirit of gentleness is our realization that each of us has been tempted and has succumbed to sin. We speak to one another gently, knowing we both need help. And we act toward one another in gentleness, for we recognize our mutual failings. We may correct. We may admonish. We may even speak with severity. But always, we must temper our response with the love and concern that is at the heart of gentleness.

The angel Gabriel, speaking to Jesus' mother, promised Mary that "the Holy Spirit will come upon you, and the power of the Most High will overshadow you" (Luke 1:35). Her Son promised the same to his disciples when he left them to rejoin the Father. We, too, can receive his promise and be clothed with "power from on high," bringing gentleness to fruition in our lives and in the lives of all we touch. With his power overshadowing us, we may now speak and act to proclaim his Kingdom and renew this world through gentleness. In our home and church, workplace and community, we, the powerless, can manifest the gentle power of the Spirit in everything we do and say.

# 14. Righteous Anger: Learning Legitimate Responses

> The anger which is selfish and uncontrolled is a sinful and hurtful thing, which must be banished from the Christian life. But the selfless anger which is disciplined into the service of Christ and our fellow men is one of the great dynamic forces of the world.
>
> —WILLIAM BARCLAY

In bearing the fruit of gentleness, anger appears oddly out of place. Every step we have taken to become gentle in character, thought, and deed seems to be in utter contradiction with our feeling and expressing anger. But there is no mistaking that anger is an essential part of the fruit of gentleness. We need only go back and examine the New Testament word for gentleness, *praotēs,* to understand this better.

Aristotle defined *praotēs* as the mean between excessive anger and excessive angerlessness. To be gentle, we must feel anger for the right reason and duration and in the right way.[1] As gentle Christians, we need to find that narrow path between becoming too angry and never acknowledging our anger.

To gain such balance in our life, we begin by looking at the Greek adjective for gentle, *praus.* Initially, this word was used to describe an animal that had been tamed and brought under control. With time, it has grown to include all those who practice the self-control over thoughts, emotions, and speech that Christ alone can give.[2] Our anger is the product of our inner nature, and letting it become Spirit-controlled is the key to stopping us from slipping from a healthy Christ-like expression of anger into its sinful use.

Born imperfect, we live our lives in conflict between the good and evil that exists within us. We remain locked in an internal struggle between our desire to serve God and to sin by disobeying his laws. And anger is no stranger to us in this never-ending warfare. In his warning to the Ephesians, Paul acknowledged that all anger isn't in violation of God's commandments, for the apostle told them to "be angry but do not sin" (Eph. 4:26).

Although we have the tendency to lump together as anger everything from rage, hostility, seething bitterness, and resentment, to physical violence, force, irritation, and frustration, several of these may have nothing to do with being sinful. Instead of automatically condemning any internal or external angry response as wrong, we need to examine each carefully in the light of the self-control that Christ imparts to us.

*Praus* means an angry response is both temperate and measured. We are utilizing the inner strength he has given us to control our passion and curb our desire to inflict pain or hurt upon another person. The emotion of anger isn't governing us; we are governing our anger instead. Our thoughts and actions aren't blind responses; they are restrained through the grace of the Holy Spirit.

Even in the heat of anger, we are able to determine what we should do and how we should respond in accordance with God's laws. Yet, as commendable as this growth may be, it still isn't enough. The self-control of being gentle insists that we then express the correct amount of anger in the correct way. Our angry words and actions must now be in harmony with God's word rather than in violation of it.

Our anger must be filtered through one more Christ-like quality for it to be a legitimate part of gentleness, and that quality is wisdom. We have to work at growing in wisdom by being willing to study Scripture and learn what God demands of us through prayer. Although blessed with common sense, we shouldn't confuse this gift with the soundness of judgment that comes with the struggle to pray for and obey God's standards in our lives. Thomas à Kempis's definition of the Christian who has this wisdom of learning and prayer rings true across the centuries: "He that is wise and well-instructed in the Spirit standeth above these mutable things; not heeding what he feeleth in himself or which way the wind of instability bloweth; but that the whole intention of his mind may tend to the proper and desired end."[3]

The proper and desired end is the wisdom to understand our anger, the strength to harness it, and the restraint to act upon our angry feelings with self-control. This is the righteous anger of *praotēs,* and nowhere was it practiced more effectively or shockingly as in Galilee and Judea during the three years of Jesus' public ministry.

## THE ANGRY SON OF GOD

The Old Testament is so replete with stories of God's wrath that we cannot help but fear his anger. We know the power of divine wrath and tremble before it. Yet, when his Son became incarnate, his anger also took on human form, responding to earthly situations in a human manner.

In studying Christ's anger, we are given a lesson in gentleness that is difficult both to decipher and to practice in our lives. The Gospels are remarkably inaccessible when we try to approach Jesus' inner thoughts and emotions. Also, the evangelists give us his words and responses in many instances without sharing the full context in which he spoke and acted.

Yet, even with these limitations, we can see that Christ expressed righteous anger clearly enough. As Michael Grant states in his excellent study of Jesus, he

did not refrain from contentiousness at all. On the contrary, he was a stormy personage with a "mighty vein of granite in his character." Arguing constantly with formidable ferocity, he gave his Jewish opponents as good as he got from them, and more. What epithets they used against Jesus we do not know. But the torrents of abuse he directed against them are recorded and cannot be dismissed as inauthentic or minimized as meaningless oriental verbiage.[4]

In the Gospel of Matthew, the Woes that are the counterpart to the Beatitudes show the full force of Jesus' anger toward the Pharisees and scribes. In these paragraphs, we read that he called them hypocrites and children of hell, blind guides and fools:

"Straining out a gnat and swallowing a camel . . . you cleanse the outside of the cup and of the plate, but inside they are full of extortion and rapacity. . . . You are like whitewashed tombs, which outwardly appear beautiful, but within they are full of dead men's bones and all uncleanness. . . . You serpents, you brood of vipers . . . " (Matt. 23:23–33).

In the Gospel of Mark, those who ignored or refused to accept Jesus' message fared little better. The money changers in the temple, the chief priests, scribes, and elders, the crowds who turned away from him, even his family and the cursed fig tree, were to varying degrees the recipients of his anger. "Even when he is said to 'sigh,' the Greek word signifies indignation rather than grief."[5]

He was on earth to usher in the dawning Kingdom of God, and those who failed to hear him and prepare themselves accordingly received the brunt of his angry words and actions. Just as his emotional and passionate human nature allowed Jesus to express a forgiving love, it also gave rise to this anger. These two feelings are not in contradiction, for we may love our friends and enemies at the same time as we rail against their hypocrisy, blasphemy, evilness, or unjust acts.

In examining Jesus' outbursts, we see that he didn't treat the unfortunate, the spiritually immature, or the defenseless angrily. More often than not, he controlled his anger with the weak but vented it on those who should have known better. The religiously well-trained yet corrupt Pharisees, the knowledgeable yet hypocritical scribes, the arrogant spiritual leaders who profited from the poverty and oppression of the Jewish people, these were the legitimate targets of his obviously strong negative emotions.

With a focused anger, Jesus declared open spiritual warfare not only on specific members of the ruling Jewish religious establishment but also on the legions of hell. He straightforwardly told the Jewish leaders, "You are of your father the devil, and your will is to do your father's desires. . . . He who is of God hears the words of God; the reason why you do not hear them is that you are not of God" (John 8:44–47).

Christ came to change us, and one of his weapons was *praotēs*, the righteous anger of gentleness. His anger was directed toward making us embrace that change of mind and heart needed for true repentance. With his declaration that the Kingdom of God had begun with him, not at some far-off date in a distant future, he showed that he wanted change to happen immediately. His task was urgent, and he displayed little tolerance of those who were used by Satan to challenge, thwart, or destroy his ministry.

As much as Jesus stressed the need for change in our minds and hearts, he didn't overlook the need to change human society also. The divine vision that leads to repentence is the same that leads to the radical activism of service. And Christ used the anger of gentleness to bring about change in society. In his ministry, revolution and repentance became united. He expressed anger toward those who would not change their hearts as well as toward those who oppressed and deprived others of their rights.

In *The Wounded Healer,* Henri Nouwen describes Jesus as a "revolutionary, Who did not become an extremist, since he did not offer an ideology, but Himself. He was also a mystic, Who did not use his intimate relationship with God to avoid the social evils of his time, but shocked his milieu to the point of being executed as a rebel."[6] As a mystic and a revolutionary, Christ used anger effectively to attack the seeds sown by the Evil One both in society and in the human heart.

## SINFUL ANGER

We, too, are to uproot the seeds sown by Satan, and we can find no better place to start than in our own hearts. To be angry without sinning, we must follow God's word as Jesus' expressed it. Our anger should become the anger of *praotēs,* neither excessive nor unexpressed. In imitation of Christ, we will use this anger constructively to draw others and ourselves closer to God and his will.

In certain ways, it is easier to begin with what this righteous and holy anger is not. *Praotēs* may be forceful, as we have seen with Jesus' overturning of the money changers' tables in the temple and his searingly honest language toward the Pharisee and scribes. But righteous anger cannot embrace violence in thought or deed. As

John Yoder concluded in *The Politics of Jesus*, "A social style charac-terized by . . . the rejection of violence of any kind is the theme of New Testament proclamation from beginning to end, from right to left."[7]

Violence is excessive anger motivated by a conscious intention to harm another person. By contrast, righteous anger springs from a God-centered desire to oppose sinful behavior, to point out evil, and to express God's will as fully as we know it.

Our anger cannot be filled with hatred of others, nor can it be based on fear of them. When one of Jesus' disciples severed the ear of the high priest's slave at the time of Christ's arrest, Jesus soundly rebuked his disciple and compassionately healed the slave. Feeling a combination of hatred and fear, the disciple had lashed out in sinful anger and found that such an action could not be justified, even though it was done in defense of the Lord. The disciple had failed to make the necessary distinction between the sinner and the sinful. Ignoring Jesus' command to love his ene-mies, this person had struck with a hostility based on his own sinfulness. His hate or fear of a slave rather than the role this man played in Jesus' arrest moved the disciple away from God's will rather than closer to it.

We may hate injustice, hate tyranny, hate greed, fear harm, fear the loss of our loved ones, fear death at the hands of others, but we must first hate and fear those very things *in* our own selves, not *in* others. And if we are to hate and fear, it cannot be a hatred or fear *of* ourselves or *of* others. We must reserve these twin emo-tions for the Evil One and the power of darkness he casts over our thoughts and actions. "Perhaps this is one reason why Jesus told us to 'turn the other cheek' and 'go the second mile,'" James Dobson states, "knowing that Satan can make devastating use of anger in an innocent victim."[8]

Uncontrolled anger is the opposite of *praotēs*. It causes harm to others, damages their self-esteem, creates bitterness, and destroys relationships. But the evilness of ungoverned anger is not limited to overt behavior. Seething subterranean feelings of anger toward others, whether they be based on self-pity, bitterness, resentment, or jealousy, are destructive to our spiritual growth and poison our relationship with God and one another.

When Paul warned the Ephesians to "not let the sun go down on your anger, and give no opportunity to the devil" (Eph. 4: 26–27), he was giving recognition to the damaging and divisive part that we allow Satan to play in our lives when we refuse to express our anger properly. The longer we let ungoverned anger thrive within us, the more bitter, self-pitying, and resentful we will grow. If our anger is harmful to others, we should take immediate action to admit to them that such anger is wrong. And even if the anger we are feeling is selflessly motivated, we mustn't repress it, giving the devil the opportunity to separate us, through our unacknowledged and unexpressed anger, from God and from one another.

In the fourth century, one of the desert mothers, Amma Syncletica, said with all the wisdom of that monastic tradition: "It is good not to get angry. But if it should happen, do not allow your day to go by affected by it, for it is said: Do not let the sun go down. Otherwise, the rest of your life may be affected by it. Why hate a person who hurts you, for it is not that person who is unjust, but the devil. Hate the sickness, but not the sick person."[9]

## CHRIST-LIKE ANGER

Imitating Christ, our anger will become the disciplined, selfless expression of *praotēs* when we learn the correct balance between venting our angry feelings and repressing them. This harmony is created within us when we move with the deliberateness that is in obedience with the biblical command to "be quick to hear, slow to speak and slow to anger" (James 1:19). Heeding this sound advice, we will find ourselves taking well-conceived and constrained steps toward positive action rather than reacting with the blind and negative rage of uncontrolled anger.

Even though Christ preached and lived a doctrine of universal and forgiving love, he also displayed a fierce and awesome anger, proving, in William Barclay's words, that "Christianity is not an easy-going tolerance which will accept anything and shut its eyes to everything. There may come a time when some battle has to be fought, and when it does, the Christian will not shirk it."[10]

Christ-like anger is used to fight, but not in the battles of earthly warfare. "What causes wars, and what causes fighting among you? Is it not your passions that are at war in your members? You desire and do not have; so you kill. And you covet and cannot obtain; so you fight and wage war" (James 4:1-2).

The warfare in which righteous anger is used is strictly spiritual; we attack those passions within ourselves and those injustices in the world to bring about change in fulfillment of God's promises. Righteous anger is one way to "fight the good fight of faith," as Paul told Timothy (1 Tim. 6:12). Again, urging his young protégé to be "a good soldier of Christ Jesus," Paul added, "no soldier on service gets entangled in civilian pursuits, since his aim is to satisfy the one who enlisted him" (2 Tim. 2:3-4).

To satisfy the One who enlisted us, we must use our anger as Christ did, concentrating it solely upon helping to usher in the Kingdom of God. Our preparation and that of others in this world should become the central principle in our lives. As Christ's disciples, we will let our anger be aroused only when our purpose is thwarted and this principle attacked.

When we see the balanced, righteous anger of *praotēs* in this light, we begin to understand that our response to the civil authorities of this world should be one of submission. But we should submit only up to the point that our obedience to civil powers is constructive and in agreement with Christian purposes and principles. When we are stopped from living our lives according to God's laws, when we are asked by our government to do that which is evil or condone evil acts, we have both a personal and a social responsibility to refuse. But our refusal is not a call to fight civil authorities so much as to resist doing wrong. Our focus needs to remain firmly fixed on the only battle engaging our efforts—the spiritual one.

"Give me a hundred men who fear nothing but God, and who hate nothing but sin, and who know nothing but Jesus Christ and him crucified, and I will shake the world," John Wesley said.[11]

Righteous anger used to serve God and one another can become a most powerful tool for change in this world. And we can do our part in this transformation by angrily resisting social evil and decay whenever and wherever we find it.

## HARNESSING ANGER

The righteous anger of *praotēs* is a nonviolent weapon with which we can arm ourselves to do spiritual battle. To harness our anger so that it is selfless and Spirit-controlled requires the considerable discipline of maintaining a consistent prayer life. It is our responsibility as gentle Christians to grow toward wholeness by taking hold of our intense negative feelings and making them become a matter of prayer.

In prayer, we open ourselves to communicating with God, hearing his advice and being led to greater understanding of the source of our anger and its Christ-like resolution. In prayer, we are taught how to couple the spirit of love with the spirit of righteous anger. We learn when to confront and rebuke, and when to forgive and show mercy. In prayer, we grow in the exercise of being controlled, realizing that by governing the intensity of our anger, God is teaching us yet another dimension of the gentleness he desires of us.

With prayer, anger becomes an opportunity to reveal *praotēs* at work in our lives. In meeting this challenge, we discover the truth in John Henry Jowett's statement, "The will of God will never lead you where the grace of God cannot keep you."[12] He is always with us, demanding yet supportive, asking yet anxious to lead us.

Even with his guidance, harnessing Christ-like anger is no easy matter for us. As is true with all our efforts to improve ourselves spiritually, we have to be willing to struggle daily with the unruly nature of our anger and to continue working to keep it under God's control. Thus harnessed, righteous anger becomes a constructive force for change. As we confront evil with our angry actions and correct our shortcomings and those of others with truthful, tempered words, our character will evolve toward ever greater maturity, and our world will move that much closer to embracing gentleness.

"The world was made as a temple, a paradise, into which God Himself would descend to dwell familiarly with the spirits He had placed there to tend it for Him," Thomas Merton wrote.[13] In deciding to discipline ourselves to act with the righteous anger of Christ, we are making ourselves and our corner of this world a more accurately gentle reflection of the One who created us and the world we tend for him.

# 15. Respect: Overcoming Public and Personal Violence

> If we communicate only that part of the gospel which corresponds to people's "felt needs" and "personal problems" (Are you lonely? Do you feel that you have failed? Do you need a friend? Then come to Jesus!) while remaining silent on their relationship to their fellow-men, on racism, exploitation and blatant injustice, we do not proclaim the gospel.
>
> —DAVID J. BOSCH

In the last chapter, we touched briefly upon the need to repudiate violence in our lives. An all-pervasive force in our society as well as in the Palestine of Jesus' time, violence is practiced on both a personal and public level in direct opposition to the values by which a gentle Christian lives. We soon learn that we cannot be both gentle and violent and still call ourselves Christians. But before we can embrace gentleness fully, we need to understand the dynamics of respect and learn how best to put it into action in our lives.

Respect is the Christ-like recognition of the dignity of others as well as freedom from faulty role, race, and sex stereotyping. Gentle Christians imbued with respect guard against becoming engaged in overt or subtle forms of domination, intimidation, exploitation, or discrimination. Recognizing that these violent traits are anathema, we, as respectful people, actively work against their expression in our personal lives and public institutions. We refuse to go along with treating others with a lack of respect, knowing that such behavior violates the dignity of our fellow human beings and perpetuates the injustice inherent in our violent society.

Respecting one another helps us to become better disciples of Christ. With respect as part of our character, we overlook the differences between human beings and look at the basis of our similarities instead. We know personal concern for others rather than aloofness, and we accept the necessity of becoming involved with others' lives as Christ did. In his life, respect for the dignity of others became the end, not the means. It was what he was, not what he had. Similarly, for us to live gentleness, we must weave respect for our fellow humans into the fiber of our character, making it an essential part of what we are.

## SENSITIVITY

There is no better starting point for examining respect than to consider these personal queries about our sensitivity toward others:

- In a highly-charged situation am I willing to listen to the voice of reason in the person who holds views contrary to mine?
- Do I resent those who oppose me? Do I feel threatened by their opposition?
- Is my manner curt and my language harsh when I am challenged by a person with a wrong opinion or attitude?
- Am I exacting and inflexible in my demands of other people?
- Am I more abrupt than caring in my daily encounters with others?
- When discussing my faith and beliefs am I dogmatic and opinionated rather than gently persuasive?
- So driven by the need to be right, do I coerce others into thinking and believing as I do through tactics that are intimidating or dominating?
- Do I judge others' weaknesses and correct their faults, rarely making allowances for their shortcomings?
- Does the rigidity of the Pharisees—or the generosity of Christ —guide me in my relationships with others?
- Are others afraid to express themselves honestly in my presence?
- Do I display my commitment as Christ's disciple in such a way that I make others feel guilty, less worthy, or inferior?

Sensitivity is ministering to others with an attentive, truly listening ear, a warm word of support, a firm yet gentle hand, a loving embrace, a tough yet tender smile, an open, flexible mind, and fairness and generosity of spirit. Sensitive relationships replace the destructive seeds of discord with more fruitful ones of caring and compassion.

When we encounter someone who has sinned, we refuse to bear false witness against them, to gossip about them or slander their name. Instead, we struggle to hold our tongue in check, and through this discipline, our sensitivity enlarges. We realize, along with Dietrich Bonhoeffer, that "God did not make this person as I would have made him. He did not give him to me as a brother for me to dominate and control, but in order that I might find above him the Creator."[1]

Rather than belittle or humiliate our brother or sister who has fallen in sin, we must acquire the sensitivity to grieve for our fellow sinner and pray for his or her repentance. We cannot know how God has fashioned the other person in his image; we can only accept that this is so and treat the other person with the sensitivity that this knowledge demands.

Refusing to speak evil of another shouldn't be confused with our legitimate responsibility to advise and guide our erring brethren. When writing to the Galatians, the apostle Paul noted that our duty to those who have sinned is to admonish them "with the spirit of gentleness" (Gal. 6:1). And that gentleness includes choosing our words sensitively and being careful that they are considerate as well as correcting, restoring as well as reproving.

Our focus now is on other people and what is best for them. But as Thomas Kelly reminds us, this growing responsibility, which we've accepted, isn't grounded "in mere humanitarianism. It is not in mere pity. It is not in mere obedience to Bible commands. It is not in anything earthly." Rather, our "social concern is the dynamic Life of God at work in the world, made special and emphatic and unique, particularized in each individual or group who is sensitive and tender in the leading-strings of love."[2]

To be sensitive and tender, we must have wide-open communion with God. Yet when we do or say something against our brethren, it will appear in our hearts at the time of prayer, effectively blocking our communication with God as it earlier blocked our communication with our fellow humans. Through insensitivity, we shut down the channels to God and one another; with tenderness, we reopen and strengthen them.

As with most spiritual lessons, we learn this one time and again on ever deeper levels of understanding and practice. So it was no surprise to me that on a recent trip to the interior of Mexico with Spanish-speaking friends, I realized such instruction of the spirit.

Staying away from the resorts usually frequented by Americans, we visited an assortment of relatives and friends, out-of-the-way shrines and open-air markets. I had difficulty understanding the rapid flow of Spanish and, after a while, found that I had begun to listen with an invisible ear, one that bypassed words and "heard" facial and other, less tangible expressions of emotion.

With wondrous clarity, I understood the devoutness of the humble pilgrim at the shrine of Father Kino, the love and pride of the young Magdalena mother of two healthy babies, and the remarkable resiliency of the ancient woman who offered us hospitality, goat's milk cheese and tortillas at her roadside home. They included me, a stranger, in the circle of their warmth, and I knew how tenderness could remove barriers of language, custom, and class and replace them with a new nondivisive spirit grounded in sensitive communication with one another and God.

Over three hundred years ago, a mystical Yorkshireman named James Nayler embraced Quakerism, suffered barbaric persecution for his controversial religious practices, and wrote several books toward the end of a life that had been filled with suffering, misunderstanding, and pain. Yet, his dying words live as an anthem to that respect we wish to incorporate into our lives today:

There is a spirit which I feel that delights to do no evil, nor to revenge any wrong, but delights to endure all things, in hope to enjoy its own in the end. Its hope is to outlive all wrath and contention, and to weary out all exaltation and cruelty, or whatever is of a nature contrary to itself. It sees to the end of all temptations. As it bears no evil in itself, so it conceives none in thoughts to any other. If it be betrayed, it bears it, for its ground and spring is the mercies and forgiveness of God. Its crown is meekness, its life is everlasting love unfeigned; it takes its kingdom with entreaty and not with contention, and keeps it by lowliness of mind.[3]

His was a sensitive voice that realized vengeful imaginings, vehement feelings, bitter reasoning, and volleys of spiteful words will reap nothing except vengeance, vehemence, bitterness, and spite. The way of respect is to remember that we stand in the presence of God wholly divested of self, doing what we can by his light and accepting what he gives us in return.

With this sensitivity as our basis for treating others with the respect they want and deserve, we renounce not only violence but also the compulsive purposes that lead us to violate the dignity of others. We begin to see each other as people more similar than dissimilar. We recognize our common anguish, suffering, hope, and joy. We understand that our disunity and separation can become unity and peace. And we long to make Christ's words a reality on this earth here and now: "I in them, and thou, Father, in me, that they may be made perfect in one. . . . And the glory which thou hast given me, I have given them, that they may be one as we also are one" (John 17:21–22). But before we can experience this unity, which is the final step in respect, we must discover what Christ-like equality means for us in our lives and examine our peace-creating role in this world.

## EQUALITY

When our words and behavior are based on class, national, racial, or social distinctions, we are not treating other people with the equality that underlies every expression of respect. By responding to people according to these distinctions, we are implying we are superior or inferior to them. Equality eliminates this sense of superiority or inferiority, attaching to each person respect based upon our common heritage as children of God.

When we meet, our response to one another should spring from this equality of respect for all of God's creatures. Our wealth or poverty, our choice of vocation or calling, skin color, age, ethnic background, sex, family name, talents, abilities, and personal taste matter little. We cannot help but see the vast range of differences among us, but we should refuse to give special privileges to or remove rights from others because of these differences. Just as brothers and sisters within a family are equal, we on this earth should live the equality of brothers and sisters within the larger family of God.

As Malcolm Muggeridge accompanied Mother Teresa on her work among the impoverished, sick, and needy in the slums of Calcutta, he was amazed to find that she "had a place in her heart for them all. To her, they are all children of God, for whom Christ died, and so deserving of all love. . . . I never experienced so perfect a sense of human equality as with Mother Teresa among her poor. Her love for them, reflecting God's love, makes them equal."[4]

If we practice the equality of Mother Teresa, we will find no room for condescension in our minds or hearts. We won't blindly stereotype people who differ from us. Nor will we discriminate against or exploit them. This equality heals the separation between people, making it possible for us to overcome our differences and celebrate our unity. It is the delicate action of grace in our soul, refusing to accept injustice and ready to take the necessary action to bring about unity.

In a letter written in the Birmingham jail during his struggle for racial equality, Martin Luther King, Jr., said, "Oppressed people cannot remain oppressed forever. . . . but [their] normal and healthy discontent can be channeled into the creative outlet of nonviolent direct action. And now this approach is being termed extremist." After calling Jesus, Amos, Martin Luther, John Bunyan, Abraham Lincoln, and Thomas Jefferson extremists for love, he then asked, "So the question is not whether we will be extremists but what kind of extremists we will be. Will we be extremists for hate or for love? Will we be extremists for the preservation of injustice or for the extension of justice? . . . Jesus Christ was an extremist for love, truth and goodness. . . . Perhaps the South, the nation and the world are in dire need of creative extremists."[5]

## PEACE-CREATORS

Another description of Martin Luther King's creative extremists would be peace-creators. These are people who not only love peace but also are willing to work to create peace. Following Christ's example, they renounce all violence, acknowledging that nothing is to be gained by such methods. They know that the object of Christianity is to bring about the Kingdom of God on earth, not through the power of human beings but by the power of God working through us. And this objective can be accomplished only by methods that are compatible with the peaceful behavior described by Christ as characteristic of those who are part of God's Kingdom.

"The Kingdom is one of peace, and the mutual greeting of his flock is a greeting of peace," wrote Dietrich Bonhoeffer in *The Cost of Discipleship*. "His disciples keep the peace by choosing to endure suffering themselves rather than inflict it on others. They maintain fellowship where others would break it off. They renounce all self-assertion, and quietly suffer in the face of hatred and wrong. In so doing, they overcome evil with good, and establish the peace of God in the midst of a world of war and hate."[6]

To understand what creators of peace are, we need only look at the words for peace in various languages around the globe. In Swahili, the word for peace, *salama,* means "without harm to soul or body." The Chinese *he ping* breaks into "harmony" *(he)* and "the absence of strife" *(ping)*. In the Malay language, *amandamai* signifies a state of peace and harmony among individuals and nations. The Japanese word *hei-wa* refers to harmonious relations marked by unity and calm, which is applied to one's thinking and to family, community, and nations. Hawaiians have several words for peace as well as a number of gestures, all indicating harmony between people united in thought. The Spanish *paz* means tranquillity and quiet and something more—the right to lead your own life while respecting the rights of others. The Russian word *mir* means peace and also village, community, world, and universe, evoking oneness.[7]

In the Hebrew word *shalom,* we find "a full-bodied concept that resonates with wholeness, unity, balance. Gathering in (but much broader than) peace, it means a harmonious, caring community with God at its center as the prime sustainer and most glorious inhabitant. This great vision of *shalom* begins and ends our Bible."[8]

In examining the language of peace, we see how much the human heart yearns for the respect, equality, unity, and wholeness that these words encompass. For creators of peace, hearts and language move beyond yearning and meet in action. These people do more than refuse to take part in war; they actively work to remove the causes of war and to repair the damage that war has done, particularly prejudice and hatred. They have accepted the gospel of Christ as their standard of behavior and struggle to live a life consistent with its peace-creating principles. These are Martin Luther King's creative extremists, for whom justice becomes a product of their respect for others and loving identification with Christ.

## TOWARD UNITY

In each of us there is a longing for unity, a half-hidden instinct to make contact with the whole of creation of which we are an infinitesimal part. We wish to move in rhythm with this world and its people, feeling a oneness with all that we can reach with our minds and hearts and senses. We want our lives touched as we have touched others' lives, and we are ready to share our loves and needs, desires and dreams without evasion. We are tired of being separated by the indifference of time and space, our own isolating blindness, and the blinding prejudice of others. We wish to acknowledge the value of others rather than focus on the sources of our division.

But to attain such unity, we must have a gentleness that is imbued with respect for all people. And that respect must be an affirmation of our spiritual dignity and equality before one another and God. Respect sees the value of the individual and the whole human family in the light of Christ, who places us in this interdependent world community and then gives us the opportunity to unite through his love and grace.

As individuals, our spiritual growth is intimately connected to our growth within society. "Our modern world cannot attain to peace, and to a fully equitable social order, merely by the application of laws which act upon man, so to speak, from outside himself," Thomas Merton warned us. "The transformation of society begins within the person. It begins with the maturing and opening out of personal freedom in relation to other freedoms—in relation to the rest of society."[9]

It means that we reach out to others with the loving openness that we would wish to receive from them. It means that we strive to meet their needs in the same way we would like ours met. It means that we desire and dream for others all that we dare to desire and dream for ourselves.

But respecting others cannot be confined to the personal realm of pure intentions, acts of charity, or goodwill. Respect carries with it a responsibility to "be effective in the context of social action, political life, work, and all the practical choices that affect our relations with others in the family, the city, the nation, and the world."[10] Respect demands that our union with God comes through our actions for others, that we serve one another as a gift to God, whose image we learn to see and respect in each other.

Only in this way can our temporal life stand in harmony with our spiritual values. In this way, too, we can bear the fruit of gentleness in ever greater abundance. Growing out of the very center of our souls, gentleness stretches out to embrace the world, proclaiming Christ's glory through our respectful attitudes and his Kingdom through our respectful deeds.

# 16. Love: Clothing Ourselves with Gentleness

And then the Lord did gently lead me along, and did let me see his love, which was endless and eternal and surpasseth all knowledge.

—GEORGE FOX

For over five hundred years in Europe, great pictorial tapestries were handwoven, serving as documentaries as well as decoration. Although this art may be traced to ancient cultures, it reached its greatest development in Gothic France, where many tapestries were created for use in religious celebrations. Favorite subjects included the Presentation of Jesus, the Legend of Saint Stephen, the Queen of Sheba, the Apocalypse, and Saint Remi. Some were composed in series, others as single panels. Size varied, too, and since they were a form of portable wealth, each was rich in texture, imagery, and craftsmanship.

These valued works of art were crafted by inserting pliant, colored wool threads called wefts into taut, stationary horizontal cotton warps. Surprisingly, the weaver never created the composition and, in fact, was legally forbidden to do so. A master artist chose the design and drew it to precise specifications, which took into account every factor, from shape to fabric color.

Learning about these beautiful creations, I soon realized why poets and songwriters down through the centuries have used the imagery of this handwoven art. Our life indeed is a tapestry, created by the divine Artist. Following his specifications, we weave the story of our life to the best of our ability, struggling always to remain faithful to the Creator's image. And in our tapestry, gentleness is the pliant, colored weft and love the stationary, yet strengthening, cotton warp. Intertwined, they express the fabric of our spiritual growth in all its richness and complexity.

The apostle Paul may have made a similar connection between gentleness and love when he wrote to the Colossians from his Roman jail cell. Colossae was a small and rather insignificant town, but it was in the center of a region known for its excellent volcanic soil and, therefore, good pasture land. Great flocks of sheep grazed on this land, and the Colossians developed a well-deserved reputation as producers of fine wool and even finer garments. They found an additional source of income in the chalky water of the region, for it was especially suitable for dyeing cloth.

When Paul made a list in his letter of the graces the Colossians should have, he used images taken directly from their workday lives as weavers and dyers: "So then, as the chosen of God, dedicated and beloved, clothe yourself with a heart of mercy, kindness, humility, gentleness. . . . And above all these clothe yourselves with love, which binds everything together in perfect harmony" (Col. 3:12–14). Love, like the cotton warp, is the permanent thread in the tapestry that is our life, through and under and around which we weave the colorful threads of our gentleness.

## THE BINDING FORCE

Full gentle life in the Spirit is both a giving and a receiving of nonpossessive, affirmative, and unselfish love involving God, others, and ourselves. Love is a force that binds us one to another and, most importantly, to God. Free of domination and control, love unites us while respecting our individuality and freedom.

As the Spirit touches us and opens our hearts to divine love, we find ourselves reaching out with the glow of that same love to those around us. And as our loving communion with God deepens, we discover all that Thomas Merton felt when he wrote:

It is in deep solitude I find the gentleness with which I can truly love my brothers. The more solitary I am the more affection I have for them. It is pure affection and filled with reverence for the solitude of others. Solitude and silence teach me to love my brothers for what they are, not for what they say.[1]

The first commandment is to love the Lord our God with all our heart, soul, strength, and mind. The second commandment is universal in application: We are to love all people. Not just our friends and beloved relatives. Not just Christians. All people. We have been commanded to love everyone as we love ourselves, no matter who they are or what they do or say. And we are to love ourselves only so that we may become agents of this love, able to respond to others' needs without selfishly expecting something in return.

This Christian love, *agape,* gathers all virtues, all graces, all fruits of the Spirit into one supreme quality in which there is no difference between belief and action. The early Christians lived *agape* in "a caring, sharing and open community that was especially sensitive to the poor and the outcast. Their love for God, for one another, and for the oppressed was central to their reputation," Jim Wallis concluded in *The Call to Conversion.* [2]

Their faith wasn't a complicated system of concepts and doctrines. They knew that the object of their faith was God and that God was Love. And in the amazing simplicity of this understanding, they could act as they believed, knowing that if they had perfect faith and no love, they were nothing (1 Cor. 13:2). With the love of God in their souls, they were made tender and loving with all they encountered.

Bound in this relationship of love with one another, the early Christians found true maturity and fulfillment. We can find this also, if we are willing to give unselfishly of ourselves to each other with spiritual concern at the heart of our sharing and caring. Loving in this way intensifies, fills, completes, and makes whole our lives. It brings us beyond egoism, beyond selfishness, beyond hatred, beyond violence, beyond hopeless struggle. Instead, we find self-giving and self-transcendence, communion and creative concern, service and strength.

## THE COLORS OF CELEBRATION

When we clothe ourselves with gentleness and bind ourselves with love, our spirits dance and our hearts sing. Drawn to God and invaded with his love, we feel our lives colored by the joyousness of these "contacts of God that wake the soul with a bound of wonder and delight, a flash of flame that blazes like an exclamation of inexpressible happiness and sometimes burns with a wound that is delectable although it gives pain."[3]

These contacts are as unexpected as they are precious, and they are to be savored in the less happy moments of our lives. But one thing is assured: We will feel the presence of his love when we most need it. The early-twentieth-century English writer John Wilhelm Rowntree discovered this to be true when his advancing blindness was confirmed by a noted physician as incurable. He left the doctor's office and was standing by the railings outside for a few moments, trying to collect his despairing thoughts, when "he suddenly felt the love of God wrap him about as though a visible presence enfolded him and joy filled him such as he had never known before."[4]

Another English mystic, William Blake, wrote simply in *Songs of Innocence/Songs of Experience* that

> Joy and woe are woven fine
> A clothing for the soul divine.

Paradoxically, both sorrow and joy come from the same divine fountain, so that at the moment of our joyous celebration, we become, like Meister Eckhart, "wet with the tears of love."[5]

In his excellent biography of Thomas Merton, Michael Mott relates a story about a tradition at the Monastery of Our Lady of Gethsemane where Merton lived. Upon the death of a monk, his fellow Trappists would greet the news with joy. When one of Merton's friends, the publisher James Laughlin, was visiting with Merton and his abbot, Dom James, their discussion of publishing plans "was interrupted by the news that one of the monks had died—both Dom James and Merton responded with alleluias." James Laughlin was astonished by their reaction and soon learned that "conflicting emotions had a part in the tradition—joy for the monk finishing his spiritual journey, sadness for those who remained on earth."[6]

In the Jewish customs that Christ followed, sorrow and joy were similarly felt, and nowhere were the contradictory emotions expressed better than in dance and song. Music was an important part of everyday Jewish life; births, weddings, and funerals were incomplete without it. In celebrating these sorrowful and happy marking points of human existence, the Jews devoted their singing and dancing to praising God's work in their lives. From the temple orchestra to the alarm trumpeted by the shophar, from the joyous sounds called for in the psalms to David's chorus of four thousand offering praises to the Lord, from the rollicking dancing to the rhythm of the timbrel at weddings to the somber steps taken to the beat of the sistrum at funerals, Jesus and his fellow Jews insisted on being both joyous and sad celebrants of life.

Today, we can color the tapestry of our life with our own sacred celebration in obedience to God's plan. And it is through the fullness of such celebration, in which joy and sorrow are woven so fine, that we approach the Kingdom of Heaven. Doing his will, we are emptied into God and transformed into celebrants of all that he is in our lives. In this way we begin to fulfill his first commandment, to love him with all our heart and all our mind and all our strength and all our spirit. And in this way, we learn, too, how to love others as ourselves. As we grow in this loving, our life as a Christian becomes less one of gloom and more one of ever increasing joy in the Lord, even in the midst of our sorrows.

Abiding in his love, we live and walk and interact with our fellow humans with that radiant love reflected in everything we do and say. We finally understand what the great teacher Origen meant when he wrote, "Because God himself has sowed and planted and given life to this seed ... it will glow and shine, gleam and burn, and it will never cease to turn toward God."[7]

This seed, our love for God and in God that reaches out to others, becomes our ground, our center, our rule, and our end. As it is given to us, we take it and labor with it. But when we bear fruit with our labor, we turn back toward God with our gift, stretching our arms to him in love, giving him the fruit of our love in celebration of that love. And with such love, we clothe ourselves with gentleness.

## THE WHOLENESS OF OUR TAPESTRY

If gentleness were woven into a tapestry of our life, it would consist of four distinct panels. Taken separately, the panels would picture each of the stages we move through in developing gentleness. Together they would represent the wholeness that can come only when we have gained true gentleness of body, mind, and spirit.

We would see the *awakening* of our soul and *surrendering* of our will, our *serving* others and our *expressing* gentleness in word and deed. We'd be able to pick out the unifying threads of commitment and devotion, fellowship and sharing. We'd discover the more difficult patterns of prayer, renunciation, obedience, and subservience. We'd immediately recognize the varied colors of humility, mercy, healing, and giving. And we'd point with wonder to the artistry of power, righteous anger, respect, and love.

Looking at the completed tapestry, we'd understand that gentleness is many things—a force, a symbol, an emotion, a ruling spirit, a display, and an act. But above all else, we'd know that gentleness is a continual process in which we can grow toward Christ-like wholeness. We would no longer feel division, estrangement, or alienation from God, others, or ourselves. Born again in Christ, and willing to die with him also, we'd celebrate his gentleness that dwells within us, shines out through us, and gathers up others into it.

Imagine our tapestry one last time, whole, complete and glowing with that fruit of the Spirit called gentleness. What would we see in this our final glance at the creation of the divine? We would see God's design and our craftsmanship, his will and our obedience, his call and our answer, his command and our fulfillment of it. We would see gentleness as we initially sought it, then struggled for it, and lastly, worked to live it in every aspect of our life. And we would know the wholeness that comes with having done our best to be faithful to the gentle Artist who creates the tapestry that is our life.

# Notes

## Introduction: To Grow in Gentleness

1. William Barclay, *The Letters to the Galatians and Ephesians* (Philadelphia: Westminster Press, 1976), p. 51.
2. Dietrich Bonhoeffer, *The Cost of Discipleship* (New York: Macmillan, 1963), p. 320.
3. David Watson, *Called & Committed: World-Changing Discipleship* (Wheaton, Ill.: Harold Shaw, 1982), p. 67.
4. George Fox, *Journal*, in *The Quaker Reader* (New York: Viking Press, 1962), p. 46–47.
5. Bonhoeffer, *Cost of Discipleship*, p. 320.
6. Meister Eckhart, *Meister Eckhart: The Essential Sermons, Commentaries, Treatises and Defenses*, trans. Edmund College and Bernard McGinn (New York: Paulist Press, 1981), p. 163.
7. Saint Augustine, *Confessions*, in *The Choice Is Always Ours* (New York: Harper & Row, 1975), p. 34.
8. François Fénelon, *Spiritual Letters to Women* (New Canaan, Conn.: Keats, 1980), p 265.
9. Wu Ming Fu, *Patterns in Jade* (New York: Avalon Press, 1935), p. 7.
10. Frederic Louis Godet, *Commentary on John's Gospel* (Grand Rapids: Kregel Publications, 1978), p. 855.
11. Thomas à Kempis, *The Imitation of Christ* (Wilton, Conn.: Morehouse-Barlow, 1981), p. 60.

## Chapter 1. Awareness: Hearing the Call

1. Thomas Lawson, quoted in Howard H. Brinton, *Friends for 300 Years* (Wallingford, Penn.: Pendle Hill, 1965), p. 217.
2. Evelyn Underhill, *The Spiritual Life*, in *The Choice Is Always Ours*, p. 79.
3. Thomas Merton, *New Seeds of Contemplation* (New York: New Directions, 1972), pp. 127–28.
4. Rufus Jones, *Social Law in the Spiritual World: Studies in Human and Divine Interrelationship* (New York: George H. Duran, 1923), p. 138.
5. Martin Buber, *Eclipse of God* (New York: Harper, 1952), p. 125.
6. George Fox, *The Quaker Reader*, p. 52.
7. Pss. 18:35; 37:11, Isa. 40:11, Zech. 9:9, Matt. 5:5; 11:29–30; 12:20, 1 Cor. 4:21, 2 Cor. 10:1, Gal. 5:22–23; 6:1, Eph. 4:2, Col. 3:12, 1 Thess. 2:7, 1 Tim. 3:3; 6:11, 2 Tim. 2:25, Titus 3:2, Heb. 5:2, James 1:21; 3:13; 3:17, 1 Pet. 5:6.
8. Merton, *New Seeds of Contemplation*, p. 3.
9. Bonhoeffer, *Cost of Discipleship*, pp. 68–69.

## Chapter 2. Openness: Being Molded Anew

1. Michael Grant, *Jesus: An Historian's Review of the Gospels* (New York: Scribner's, 1977), p. 50.
2. William Law, *A Serious Call to a Devout and Holy Life* (Wilton, Conn.: Morehouse-Barlow, 1982), p. 39.
3. Merton, *New Seeds of Contemplation,* p. 157.
4. *Interpreter's Dictionary of the Bible,* vol. 3 (Nashville: Abingdon Press, 1962), p. 334; Charles L. Allen, *God's Psychiatry* (Old Tappan, N.J.: Fleming H. Revel, 1953), p. 137.
5. Paul Tillich, *The New Being* (New York: Scribner's, 1955), p. 15. I am indebted to John H. Yoder for the following explanation of Paul's use of New Creation upon which Tillich bases this statement. In *The Politics of Jesus* (Grand Rapids: Eerdmans, 1972), Yoder argues that a careful translation of the Greek *ktisis* for creation shows that Paul meant a new social reality, not necessarily a transformed and renewed individual. This interpretation changes and broadens our perspective, with emphasis now placed on the new world, which begins in Christ.
6. Gerald Heard, *The Creed of Christ* (New York: Harper & Row, 1940), p. 24.
7. Francis A. Schaeffer, *True Spirituality* (Wheaton, Ill.: Tyndale House, 1983), p. 18.
8. William Penn, *Fruits of an Active Life,* in *The Quaker Reader,* p. 425.
9. Tillich, *The New Being,* p. 22.
10. Eckhart, *Meister Eckhart,* p. 292.
11. Merton, *New Seeds of Contemplation,* p. 71.


## Chapter 3. Devotion: Exploring the Kingdom of God Within

1. Barclay, *Letters to the Galatians and Ephesians,* p. 51.
2. Thomas R. Kelly, *A Testament of Devotion* (New York: Harper & Row, 1941), p. 31.
3. François Fénelon, *Christian Perfection* (Minneapolis: Bethany House, 1975), pp. 29, 76.
4. Robert Barclay, in *The Quaker Reader,* p. 229.
5. Kelly, *Testament of Devotion,* p. 31.
6. Henri J. M. Nouwen, *Reaching Out* (Garden City, N.Y.: Doubleday, 1975), p. 25.
7. Brother Lawrence, *The Practice of the Presence of God* (Old Tappan, N.J.: Fleming H. Revell, 1958), p. 8.
8. George Fox, *Journal,* as quoted in Howard Brinton's *Friends for 300 Years,* p. 76.
9. Kelly, *Testament of Devotion,* p. 32.
10. Hannah Whitall Smith, in *The Quaker Reader,* p. 390. Thomas Merton, *No Man Is an Island* (Garden City, N.Y.: Doubleday, 1967), p. 174. François Fénelon, *Fénelon's Spiritual Letters* (Augusta, Maine: Christian Books, 1982), p. 141. Dietrich Bonhoeffer, *Life Together* (San Francisco: Harper & Row, 1954), p. 59.
11. Fénelon, *Fénelon's Spiritual Letters,* p. 27.
12. Thomas Merton, in *A Thomas Merton Reader,* ed. Thomas P. McDonnell (Garden City, N.Y.: Doubleday, 1974), p. 292.

13. Dom John Chapman, *Spiritual Letters of Dom John Chapman,* in *The Choice Is Always Ours,* p. 237.
14. Watson, *Called And Committed,* p. 105.
15. Merton, *No Man Is an Island,* p. 164.
16. Kelly, *Testament of Devotion,* p. 122.
17. Merton, *New Seeds of Contemplation,* p. 3.
18. Ibid., p. 216.
19. Margaret Fell, in *The Quaker Reader,* p. 219.
20. Kelly, *Testament of Devotion,* p. 122.
21. Elizabeth Hunter, in *The Choice Is Always Ours,* p. 285.
22. Brother Lawrence, *Practice of the Presence of God,* p. 27.
23. Richard Foster, *Celebration of Discipline: The Path to Spiritual Growth* (San Francisco: Harper & Row, 1978), p. 90.
24. Fénelon, *Fénelon's Spiritual Letters,* p. 239.

## Chapter 4. Belonging: Going Where Gentleness Is

1. C. S. Lewis, *Mere Christianity* (New York: Macmillan, 1943), p. 144.
2. Merton, *New Seeds of Contemplation,* p. 77.
3. Ronald J. Sider, *Rich Christians in an Age of Hunger* (Downers Grove, Ill.: InterVarsity Press, 1977), p. 164.
4. Foster, *Celebration of Discipline,* p. 138.
5. Jessamyn West, in *The Quaker Reader,* p. 250.
6. John Woolman, in Howard Brinton's *Friends for 300 Years,* p. 68.
7. Bonhoeffer, *Life Together,* p. 30.
8. William Barclay, *More New Testament Words* (London: SCM, 1948), p. 16.
9. Kelly, *Testament of Devotion,* p. 82.
10. Watson, *Called & Committed,* p. 23.

## Chapter 5. Surrender: Submitting Our Will to God

1. Barclay, *Letters to the Galatians and Ephesians,* p. 51.
2. Fénelon, *Spiritual Letters to Women,* p. 117.
3. Ibid., p. 68.
4. Fénelon, *Christian Perfection,* p. 66.
5. Merton, *New Seeds of Contemplation,* p. 200.
6. Fénelon, *Fénelon's Spiritual Letters,* pp. 134–35.
7. Thomas Merton, *Thoughts in Solitude* (New York: Farrar Straus Giroux, 1956), p. 34.
8. David E. Rosage, *Follow Me* (Ann Arbor, Mich.: Servant Books, 1982), p. 59.
9. Merton, *New Seeds of Contemplation,* p. 258.
10. Brinton, *Friends for 300 Years,* p. 35.
11. Bonhoeffer, *Cost of Discipleship,* p. 47.

## Chapter 6. Renunciation: Giving All Rights to God

1. Barclay, *Letters to the Galatians and Ephesians*, p. 52.
2. Bonhoeffer, *Cost of Discipleship*, pp. 122–23.
3. Eckhart, *Meister Eckhart*, p. 198.
4. Augustine, quoted in Eckhart, *Meister Eckhart*, p. 292.
5. Ibid., p. 197.
6. Bonhoeffer, *Cost of Discipleship*, pp. 122–23.
7. Fénelon, *Fénelon's Spiritual Letters*, p. 205.
8. Merton, *No Man Is an Island*, p. 89.
9. Andrew Murray, *Absolute Surrender* (Chicago: Moody Press, 1983), p. 112.
10. Bonhoeffer, *Cost of Discipleship*, p. 102.
11. Thomas à Kempis, *Imitation of Christ*, p. 19.
12. Fénelon, *Spiritual Letters to Women*, p. 247.
13. Law, *A Serious Call to a Devout and Holy Life*, p. 44.
14. Merton, *New Seeds of Contemplation*, p. 203.
15. Bonhoeffer, *Cost of Discipleship*, p. 289.
16. Merton, *New Seeds of Contemplation*, p. 203.
17. Saint Theresa, in *The Choice Is Always Ours*, pp. 290–91.
18. Merton, *New Seeds of Contemplation*, p. 193.

## Chapter 7. Obedience: Yielding Our Life to God

1. Kelly, *Testament of Devotion*, p. 61.
2. Evelyn Underhill, *Mysticism*, in *The Choice Is Always Ours*, p. 231.
3. Bonhoeffer, *Cost of Discipleship*, p. 90.
4. Watson, *Called & Committed*, p. 103.
5. Merton, *New Seeds of Contemplation*, p. 260.
6. Fénelon, *Fénelon's Spiritual Letters*, pp. 163–64.
7. Kelly, *Testament of Devotion*, p. 71.
8. Ibid., pp. 97–98.
9. Fénelon *Christian Perfection*, p. 76.
10. Bonhoeffer, *Cost of Discipleship*, pp. 73–74.
11. Watson, *Called & Committed*, p. 177.

## Chapter 8. Subservience: Doing God's Will

1. Foster, *Celebration of Discipline*, p. 101.
2. Yoder, *Politics of Jesus*, p. 181.
3. Fénelon. *Fénelon's Spiritual Letters*, p. 26.
4. Johannes Hammel, quoted in Yoder, *Politics of Jesus*, p. 184.
5. John Woolman, in *The Quaker Reader*, p. 270.
6. Merton, *New Seeds of Contemplation*, p. 103.
7. Bonhoeffer, *Cost of Discipleship*, p. 289.
8. Allan A. Hunter, *Three Trumpets Sounded*, in *The Choice Is Always Ours*, p. 427.

9. Eckhart, *Meister Eckhart,* p. 250.
10. Fénelon, *Fénelon's Spiritual Letters,* pp. 190–91.

## Chapter 9. Humility: Joining the Poor in Spirit

1. John Selden, *Table Talk,* in John Bartlett's *Familiar Quotations,* (Boston: Little, Brown, 1980), p. 263.
2. T. S. Eliot, *Shakespeare and the Stoicism of Seneca* (New York: Harcourt, Brace and World, 1935), p. 27.
3. Jerry Bridges, *The Practice of Godliness* (Colorado Springs: NavPress, 1983), p. 221.
4. Thomas à Kempis, *Imitation of Christ,* pp. 11–12.
5. Fénelon, *Christian Perfection,* p. 205.
6. Merton, *New Seeds of Contemplation,* p. 189.
7. Bonhoeffer, *Life Together,* p. 99.
8. Ibid, p. 99.
9. Grant, *Jesus,* p. 60.
10. Ibid, p. 61.
11. Eckhart, *Meister Eckhart,* p. 199.
12. Yushi Nomura, *Desert Wisdom: Sayings of the Desert Fathers* (Garden City, N.Y.: Doubleday, 1984), pp. 20–21.
13. Merton, *New Seeds of Contemplation,* p. 190.
14. Nomura, *Desert Wisdom,* p. 77.

## Chapter 10. Mercy: Shouldering the Cheerful Burden

1. Tillich, *New Being,* pp. 7–8.
2. Bonhoeffer, *Life Together,* p. 93.
3. Quoted from "Practicing Mercy—Without Permission," William Sloane Coffin, *USA Today,* October 28, 1985.
4. Eckhart, *Meister Eckhart,* p. 226.
5. Elizabeth Fry, in *The Quaker Reader,* p. 302.
6. Ibid, p. 302.

## Chapter 11. Healing: Ministering to Body, Mind, and Spirit

1. Allen, *God's Psychiatry,* p. 9.
2. Richard F. Lovelace, *Dynamics of Spiritual Life* (Downers Grove, Ill.: InterVarsity Press, 1979), p. 256.
3. Grant, *Jesus,* p. 33.
4. C. F. Evans, quoted in Grant, *Jesus,* p. 31.
5. Watson, *Called & Committed,* p. 127.

6. Kelsey, *Other Side of Silence*, p. 71.
7. Rufus Jones, *The Trail of Life in College* (New York: Macmillan, 1929), p. 160.
8. Ibid, p. 160.
9. Kelsey, *Other Side of Silence*, p. 36.
10. Watson, *Called & Committed*, p. 70.
11. Dennis Linn and Matthew Linn, *Healing Life's Hurts: Healing Memories Through the Five Stages of Forgiveness* (New York: Paulist Press, 1978), p. 52.
12. Foster, *Celebration of Discipline*, p. 137.
13. Tillich, *New Being*, pp. 44–45.
14. Nomura, *Desert Wisdom*, p. 53.
15. William Hendriksen, *The Gospel of Matthew* (Grand Rapids: Baker Book House, 1973), p. 504.

## Chapter 12. Giving: Developing a Practical Covenant

1. Johannes Jorgensen, *St. Francis of Assisi* (New York: Doubleday, 1955), pp. 33–39.
2. Eckhart, *Meister Eckhart*, pp. 275–76.
3. Nouwen, *Reaching Out*, p. 47.
4. Ibid., p. 47.
5. Dominique Lapierre, *The City of Joy*, trans. Kathryn Spink (Garden City, N.Y.: Doubleday, 1985), pp. 28–29.
6. Jorgensen, *St. Francis of Assisi*, p. 37.
7. Nomura, *Desert Wisdom*, pp. 36–37.
8. Kelly, *Testament of Devotion*, p. 74.
9. Merton, *No Man Is an Island*, p. 86.
10. The subject of stewardship, sharing, and caring is immensely complex, and, by necessity, this discussion must be brief. For more information, I strongly recommend Richard J. Foster's *Freedom of Simplicity* (San Francisco: Harper & Row, 1981).
11. Watson, *Called & Committed*, p. 77.

## Chapter 13. Power: Carrying Out the Charge

1. Kelly, *Testament of Devotion*, pp. 41–42.
2. Law, *Serious Call to a Devout and Holy Life*, p. 58.
3. Tillich, *The New Being*, p. 90.
4. Watson, *Called & Committed*, p. 81.
5. Bridges, *Practice of Godliness*, p. 221.
6. Henri J. M. Nouwen, *A Cry for Mercy: Prayers from the Genesee* (Garden City, N.Y.: Doubleday, 1983), p. 109.
7. Kelly, *Testament of Devotion*, p. 47.
8. Thomas Merton, *Love and Living*, ed. Naomi Burton Stone and Brother Patrick Hart (New York: Farrar Straus Giroux, 1979), p. 156.
9. Kelly, *Testament of Devotion*, p. 48.

10. Merton, *No Man Is an Island,* p. 97.
11. Bridges, *Practice of Godliness,* p. 224.

## Chapter 14. Righteous Anger: Learning Legitimate Responses

1. Grant, *Jesus,* p. 217.
2. Barclay, *Letters to the Galatians and the Ephesians,* p. 52.
3. Thomas à Kempis, *Imitation of Christ,* p. 48.
4. Grant, *Jesus,* p. 76.
5. Ibid., p. 77.
6. Henri J. M. Nouwen, *The Wounded Healer* (Garden City, N.Y.: Doubleday, 1972), pp. 20–21.
7. Yoder, *Politics of Jesus,* p. 250.
8. James Dobson, *Emotions: Can You Trust Them?* (Ventura, Calif.: Regal Books, 1980), p. 92.
9. Nomura, *Desert Wisdom,* p. 84.
10. William Barclay, *Letters to the Romans* (Philadelphia: Westminster Press, 1975), p. 170.
11. Barclay, *Letters to the Galatians and the Ephesians,* p. 156.
12. John Henry Jowett, quoted in Dobson, *Emotions,* p. 104.
13. Merton, *New Seeds of Contemplation,* p. 290.

## Chapter 15. Respect: Overcoming Public and Personal Violence

1. Bonhoeffer, *Life Together,* p. 93.
2. Kelly, *Testament of Devotion,* pp. 110–11.
3. James Nayler, in *A Quaker Reader,* p. 129.
4. Malcolm Muggeridge, *Something Beautiful for God: Mother Teresa of Calcutta* (Garden City, N.Y.: Doubleday, 1977), p. 19.
5. Martin Luther King, Jr., *Why We Can't Wait* (New York: Harper & Row, 1963), pp. 68–69.
6. Bonhoeffer, *Cost of Discipleship,* p. 126.
7. These definitions were taken from "Ideas and Words for 'Peace' Vary with Cultures," Joseph A. Murphy, *Albuquerque Journal,* December 2, 1985.
8. Foster, *Freedom of Simplicity,* p. 30.
9. Merton, *Love and Living,* pp. 154–55.
10. Ibid., p. 154.

## Chapter 16 Love: Clothing Ourselves with Gentleness

1. Thomas Merton, *The Sign of Jonas* (New York: Harcourt, Brace, 1953), p. 261.
2. Jim Wallis, *The Call to Conversion: Recovering the Gospel for These Times* (San Francisco: Harper & Row, 1981), p. 14.

3. Merton, *New Seeds of Contemplation*, p. 277.

4. John Wilhelm Rowntree, in Kelly, *Testament of Devotion*, p. 94.

5. Eckhart, *Meister Eckhart*, p. 195.

6. Michael Mott, *The Seven Mountains of Thomas Merton* (Boston: Houghton Mifflin, 1984), p. 461.

7. Origen, *Homilies on Genesis*, in Eckhart, *Meister Eckhart*, p. 241.

# INDEX